OUR POLITICAL PARADOX

FRANK M. MARTIN

It could probably be shown by facts and figures that there is no distinctly native American criminal class except Congress.

—**Mark Twain**

Critical thinking: the real national debt.

—**Unknown author**

ISBN: 1494465329
ISBN 13: 9781494465322
Library of Congress Control Number: 2013923206
CreateSpace Independent Publishing Platform
North Charleston, South Carolina

CONTENTS

CONTENTS

INTRODUCTION

The political culture in the United States has become such a dichotomy that both the extreme Left and the extreme Right have entrenched themselves with such determination that it has encumbered any hopes for reasonability. Political parties are *not* sports teams that one can immeasurably and unconditionally support; perhaps that's where it is all going wrong. For example, I love the shooting sports such as skeet, United States Pistol Shooter's Association Pistol Competitions , and hunting, to name a few; yet I truly find it ironic that in the United States it is a constitutional right to bear arms but not to have health care. Last time I checked, one has to be alive, and preferably healthy, to enjoy all our freedoms—particularly shooting—or it's a "dead" issue. Even more ironic is that many want small government, yet the value of the US dollar is tied to the full faith and trust in our government. The extreme Left wants government, for the most part, to sustain them, while the extreme right wants a bucket-size government; and there is no real plan or formula to reach a compromise from both sides.

The paradox of our political culture is that each party feels that their party's philosophy is what's best for our country and the same applies to many voters who are staunch supporters of their party and only research information that concurs with their view and party's philosophy. Throughout this book, I will provide examples of this nefarious element of our political culture that we must change, as it continues to pepper the very core of our great country.

When research is done without contrasting information, nothing is achieved or proven; but human nature being what it is, we seek approval and those who are like us.

I have written this book not to change anyone's political views but instead to encourage as many Americans to do what is best for us as a country; to learn to do research, understand our individual needs and our country's need, and vote accordingly and with purpose, not *fanaticism* . I hope to spark an interest for all of you to inform yourselves not just about current events but also with all events in the past that have led us to where we are today.

Our approach must be eclectic in order to add to, not detract from, our country's—and ultimately our own—best interests. In today's information era, there is no excuse to not do research. As Charlton Heston said when he was president of the National Rifle Association, "If they took a few minutes to do some research, they would have known...." Well, his statement applies to everything we do; we need to get in habit of doing our homework and stop relying on the perspectives of others simply because we opt to select the path of least resistance.

All the information contained in this book has been acquired from the Internet and—trust me—the vast majority of what I am about to tell you is surprisingly easy to acquire with a few simple keystrokes on any computer that has Internet access. In fact, do not just research what I state in this book solely based on my assertions; take on your own inquiry and more likely than not you too will find the same articles that will concur with the statements as well as others that will add, detract, and even refute what I am saying. The key lies in your ability to understand, analyze, and comprehend the subject matter, and you should come to your own conclusions based on your own research.

We, regardless of political affiliation, are facing hard and challenging times, and I am fairly certain that you will agree with me that information, education, and our ability to learn and act on what we learn will help us to great measure. I do not think that being eclectic in what you read, hear, and see will affect you in an adverse way. Some may argue that it will simply confuse you, and it may, but then again it is up to you to further your research, and one of these things may happen: it'll support your view, change your view, or—heaven forbid—you might learn something new.

I challenge you to not just read and accept what I say in this book but to research and see for yourself what you can do to inform yourself and add, detract, or contest what is being said—and use that to your benefit. Additionally, I have purposely authored this book to be a short and easy read with the intention that it will instigate you to do more reading and research on your own; I am quite sure that this book can be read in one sitting.

Furthermore, it is not my intent to even speculate that my views have the "answers" to our nation's issues but, to the best of my knowledge and in my current situation and how it interacts with my community and ultimately our country, I am fairly certain that an informed voter will feel better about his or her choices.

We have many wonderful freedoms in the United States, and I have traveled enough to say that there is no other place in this world that I would rather live; it truly is our country and we owe it to ourselves, our children, and our fellow Americans—regardless of political views—to vote diligently and as well-informed citizens.

Finally, I want to thank you for purchasing this book. The proceeds will go to pay for my student loans and to fund another book about our future political candidates.

CHAPTER 1

OUR POLITICAL SYSTEM

In the United States our political structure comprises a federal constitutional republic where the president of the United States is the head of state and of the government. Congress, along with the judiciary branch, shares powers of the national government where the federal government shares sovereignty with state governments. All of this occurs through general elections which take place within a two-party system regardless of the fact that a two-party system is not statutorily required, otherwise new parties would not emerge.

Furthermore, our government consists of three branches, each of which runs independently: the executive branch, headed by the president; the legislative branch, vested in a binary chamber system that is comprised of the Senate and the House of Representatives; and the judicial branch, composed of the Supreme Court and lesser-ranked federal courts. These courts are charged with interpreting the US Constitution, federal laws, and other federal regulations. Within this scope, their primary functions are the resolution of disputes between the executive and legislative branches. Our government's parameters are delineated by the Constitution. While there have been other political parties in the United States, the two most common and enduring are the Democratic Party and the Republican Party. Whereas most of us are governed by state laws and those of other political subdivisions, such as county and city, the US Constitution delineates our overall governmental structure.

The historical fact is that the federal government was created by the states as colonies were established individually and self-governed, each independent of the others. Local governments were created to effectively carry out functions for the respective states. New states were admitted and molded accordingly into the Union.

CHAPTER 2

THE HISTORY OF OUR POLITICAL PARTIES

During the early years of our country, the Democratic-Republican Party (DRP) emerged from the anti-Federalist movement that opposed the fiscal policies of Alexander Hamilton in the early 1790s; the party was organized by James Madison and Thomas Jefferson.

The DRP supported states' rights and strict compliance with the US Constitution; it opposed national bank and wealth interests. It ascended to power in the election of 1800, and after the War of 1812 the Federalist Party (the DRP's rival) disbanded.

The Democratic Party's History

Intrinsic conflicts regarding the choice for the successor of then president James Monroe, along with a sector that backed many of the Jeffersonian principles, whose biggest proponents were Andrew Jackson and Martin Van Buren, later led to a split in the DRP, and thus the rise of the Democratic Party. The Democratic Party and the Whig Party were the predominant parties in the United States until the Civil War. The Whig Party was a "commercial" party, was considerably less popular, and had limited financial support. Divided by the slavery issue and the Mexican-American War, the Whig Party simply faded away into history. During the 1850s under the cloud and weight of the Fugitive Slave Law and the Kansas-Nebraska Act, antislavery Democrats left the party and joined former members of the remaining parties, thus giving birth to the Republican Party.

The "reorganized" Democratic Party was left with much internal turmoil with the choice of a successor to President James Buchanan, in addition to the division of the North and South. The Republican Party organized and ultimately won the election of 1860 with its candidate, Abraham Lincoln. As if the Democratic Party was not in enough disarray, the Civil War commenced; the Democrats were divided into the "War Democrats" and the "Peace Democrats." In all of this, the Confederate States of America did not have any political parties, viewing them as malevolent factions that they were better off not supporting. The majority of the War Democrats supported Abraham Lincoln and the Republican Party.

In 1864, Andrew Johnson was on the ticket as a Democrat from the South, and in 1865 he replaced President Abraham Lincoln while remaining neutral to both the Republican Party and the Democratic Party. Ironically, the Democratic Party benefited from the South's resentment of the Reconstruction Era and hostility to the Republican Party. After the end of Reconstruction in the 1870s and the violent disfranchisement of African Americans took place in the 1890s, the Southern Democrats became the largest bloc of voters. The South became known as the "Solid South." Notwithstanding the fact that the Republicans won most of the presidential elections, the Democrats somehow stayed competitive. Regardless, the Democratic Party was profuseness; the Bourbon Democrats, led by Samuel J. Tilden and

Grover Cleveland (the latter was elected for two nonconsecutive terms as president in 1889 and 1892), were representatives of large business entities such as mercantile, banking, and railroad interests. They were opponents of imperialism and overseas expansion, and supported gold standards, and opposed high tariffs and taxes.

Through the efforts of the Agrarian Democrats in 1896, the Bourbon Democrats were ousted; this was followed by the nomination of William Jennings Bryan for the presidency, which was repeated in 1900 and 1908. Throughout this period a spirited campaign was set in motion protesting eastern state financial interests, but still the Republican William McKinley won the presidency. In 1910, the Democrats took control of the House of Representatives and Woodrow Wilson was elected president in 1912 and again in 1916. Wilson led congress to address the issues of tariffs that lasted for forty years. However, in 1929 the Great Depression began while Republican president Herbert Hoover, along with a Republican Congress, set the stage for a more liberal movement within the government. Ironically, the Democrats maintained successive control of the House of Representatives for the better part of sixty years and won most presidential elections through 1968.

In 1932, Franklin D. Roosevelt was elected president and initiated the New Deal, which initiated liberal measures to promote labor unions, business regulations, civil rights, and welfare programs. Stressing long-term growth, opponents to this endeavor trenched themselves in support of businesses and demanded long-term growth and called themselves "Conservatives," felt that these liberal measures would encumber business' long term growth. Both parties were forced to address many issues arising from World War II, the Cold War, and the civil rights movement based on the demands and actions of US citizens. Republicans, however, attracted conservative and white Southerners from Democratic ranks in opposition to the New Deal and Great Society liberalism and the in favor of the Republican

Southern Strategy. African Americans, who for the most part were Republicans, commenced to migrate following the Roosevelt administration's New Deal along with the civil rights movement. At this point in time, the Democratic Party's support came from the Northeast. Bill Clinton was elected in 1992, the first Democratic president since Jimmy Carter had suffered a drastic loss to Ronald Reagan in 1980. In 1994, the Democrats lost control of Congress to the Republicans. President Clinton was reelected in 1996, making him the first Democrat since Franklin Roosevelt to be reelected. In 2006, the Democrats regained control of both the House and the Senate, only to lose control of the House in 2010 along with that of state legislatures and governorships.

Sources:

Democratic National Committee, "About Our History," http://www.democrats.org/about/our_history, accessed 4/22/2012

"History of the Democratic Party," http://www.essortment.com/history-democratic-party-60831.html, accessed 04/22/2012

"http://www.wasatchwatcher.com/history-democratic-party.html, accessed 04/22/2012.

The Republican Party

The Republican Party is commonly known as the Grand Old Party (GOP). From the time it ran its first presidential candidate, John C. Fremont, in 1856 (who didn't win), to president George W. Bush, who was in office until 2008, the party has had presidents in the White House for 84 of those 148 years. Commonly, the Republican Party's strength came from the Northeast and the Midwest. Following World War II, its support began to propagate through the South and the West. Until recently, the Republican Party was the more conservative of the two parties, but with the birth of the Tea Party movement within the Republican Party, the latter has taken the lead in conservatism. Yet the GOP still draws support throughout the upper middle class, corporations, financial concerns, and some farmers. Often the GOP stands in favor of free enterprise and fiscal responsibility and in opposition to welfare theories and practices. This is in support of the theory that smaller government is better government and limited involvement of government in both business and individuals' concerns is better.

The Republican Party emerged out of slavery's expansion into the nation's western territories and the oscillating conflicts of the opposition to slavery. The stimulus for its founding was the passage of the Kansas-Nebraska Act of 1854, which established laws that rescinded previous accords that excluded slavery from the territories. This act was an attempt to unify the abolitionists and to polarize the Democrats and the Whigs. One well-known movement that it sparked was the "anti-Nebraska" protest meetings that spread like wildfire through the country. These meetings were attended by free soldiers, Democrats, and Whigs who decided to call themselves Republicans because they were descendants of Thomas Jefferson's Democratic - Republican Party. The name Republican was officially adopted in a convention in Jackson, Michigan, on July 6, 1854, and in 1858 the Republicans won control of the House of Representatives.

Perhaps the Republicans' best known American icon was Abraham Lincoln, who earned the presidential nomination during the Republican national convention in 1860. The platform included issues such as pledging not to expand slavery, the enactment of free-homestead legislation, and the establishment of mail service, a trans-continental railroad, and a protective tariff.

When Abraham Lincoln was elected with 39.8 percent of the popular vote, running against Northern Democrat Stephen Douglas and Southern Democrat John Cabell, he had earned nearly half a million more votes than Stephen Douglas, even though the votes were just about split in thirds.

With the end of the Civil War came President Lincoln's assassination, but the Republican Party continued dominating the US political landscape, starting with president Ulysses S. Grant; this domination lasted the better part of seventy years (with occasional Democratic victories).

In 1876 Rutherford B. Hays of Ohio was nominated and the Republican Party was reunited with Hays's promises of civil service reform and to withdraw troops from the South. In general, President Hays's administration was successful in ending Reconstruction and finalizing civil reform. Hays did not seek reelection, however, and James A. Garfield was nominated as the Republican candidate in 1880 with Chester A. Arthur as the vice presidential nominee. Garfield won election by a narrow margin, but was assassinated only six months into his term. Arthur became the president; he successfully passed the Pendleton Act, which created a civil service based on merit. Chester A. Arthur failed to summon support from his party, becoming the only sitting president to be denied re-nomination by the Republican Party. Instead, James C. Blaine of Maine received the nomination and ran against Democrat Grover Cleveland of New York in 1884. This campaign became known as one of the most corrupt and dirtiest in history, with Cleveland narrowly winning.

Republican Benjamin Harrison defeated Cleveland by an electoral vote of 233 to 168, and he became famous for passing the Sherman Antitrust Act. Furthermore, during President Harrison's term several states were introduced to the Union and passed the highly protective McKinley Tariff Act. President Harrison was renominated in 1892, yet lost to Grover Cleveland.

In 1896, William McKinley earned the Republican nomination with the support of a vast popular majority, thus giving the Republicans renewed hope; the foundation of this support was the business community. The Democrats, however, had the support of agricultural areas, the South, and the labor community.

The McKinley administration was known for its role in the Spanish-American War (1898) and the acquisition of Guam, the Philippines, Cuba and Puerto Rico, along with the annexation of Hawaii, thus giving the United States an increasing presence in world politics. However, Cuba refused the US's encumbrance and through the Platt Amendment Cuba became completely independent.

President McKinley won reelection against William Jennings Bryan, only to be assassinated in September 14, 1901. Theodore Roosevelt was sworn in as president, which was the beginning of a remarkable era in American politics.

Under the Roosevelt administration, the United States witnessed reforms in economic, political, and social realms, to name a few. Among the most remarkable reforms were wildlife conservation and the implementation of Roosevelt's trust-busting ideas. In 1908, as he had promised, Roosevelt did not seek reelection; William Howard Taft from Ohio was nominated and defeated William Jennings Bryan's third attempt to run for president. Ironically, in 1912 Roosevelt challenged Taft for the nomination. Unable to win, Roosevelt broke ranks with the Republicans and ran as a Progressive Party candidate. With the dilution of the Republican Party's votes, Democrat Woodrow Wilson won the 1912 election by an overwhelming majority.

The Republicans nominated Supreme Court justice Charles E. Hughes in 1916 to run against Wilson, but Wilson's domestic record and his pledge to keep the United States out of the European war proved to be far too great for Charles Evans Hughes to overcome in order to win the election. Notwithstanding President Wilson's promise to keep the United States out of World War I, the United States was drawn into the war and politics, as usual, gave way to bipartisan practices in the action of the war. However, all was not lost; the Republicans won control of both the Senate and the House of Representatives.

In 1920, the Republican ticket of Warren G. Harding and Calvin Coolidge won by a landslide. President Harding's administration was plagued by scandals that were ultimately inherited by Coolidge after Harding died in Oregon while traveling to Alaska in 1923. In an effort put an end to these scandals, Coolidge appointed two prosecutors, one from each party, to handle them. In 1924 he was reelected by a large margin.

In 1928, with Coolidge's opting not to run for reelection, the Republican Party turned to Herbert Hoover from California. Hoover won overwhelmingly over Alfred E. Smith, and the Republicans once again won both the House of Representatives and Senate. While Hoover was reelected in 1932 in the midst of the Great Depression of the 1930s, Franklin Delano Roosevelt defeated Hoover with just as an impressive win as when Hoover had defeated Alfred E. Smith. The seventy-year reign of the Republican Party had ostensibly come to an end. Perhaps one of President Roosevelt's greatest accomplishments was attracting African American votes away from the Republicans.

The nomination of general Dwight D. Eisenhower by the Republican Party in 1952 was the result of one of the most widely divided conventions. The Republican Party was split between Eisenhower and Robert A. Taft from Ohio for the nomination. However, Eisenhower did win by a landslide victory, carrying thirty-nine states. The victory in 1956 with the Eisenhower and Nixon ticket was just as successful in winning reelection, but Democratic Party maintained control of both the Senate and the House of Representatives after the election of 1954.

In 1960, Vice President Nixon won the presidential nomination of the Republican Party effortlessly. However, he lost the election to John F. Kennedy from Massachusetts by the narrowest of margins: 113,000 votes out of more than 68 million cast.

With a bitter intrinsic party struggle preceding the 1964 Republican Convention, senator Barry M. Goldwater from Arizona wrested the presidential nomination and control of the Party from Eastern moderates and commenced an attempt to make the Republican Party well entrenched in purely conservative ideology. Yet the landslide winning of the election by Lyndon B. Johnson seemed so deplorable that it left the Republican Party in total disarray.

In 1969 Richard Nixon, with Maryland governor Spiro T. Agnew as his running mate, went on to win the election against Democrat Hubert H. Humphrey, who attempted to keep his party together after the polarization of its ranks over the Vietnam War. President Nixon will be remembered for his success in improving relations with China and the Soviet Union, an improved economy, and perceived peace in Vietnam. In the elections of 1972, Nixon won reelection against Democratic nominee George S. McGovern from South Dakota. The landslide victory included the District of Columbia and all states with the exception of Massachusetts; however, the Democrats continued their control of both houses of Congress. However, the political scandal of the burglary of the Democratic National Committee headquarters in the Watergate office complex led to the revelations of civil and criminal malfeasance within Republican campaign organization and the Nixon White House. Impeachment was inevitable, and Nixon ultimately resigned in 1974. In 1973 Vice President Agnew was forced to resign after being convicted of income tax evasion; Gerald R. Ford became his successor, thus becoming president upon Nixon's resignation.

President Ford's administration faced chronic unemployment, high interest rates, high inflation, and enormous budget deficits largely due to the cost of the Vietnam War. Ford's was criticized for having made insufficient efforts to remedy the nation's economic state, for proposing amnesty for Vietnam-era draft evaders and, above all, for the appointment of Nelson Rockefeller as his vice president. Consequently, Ford lost the election to Democrat Jimmy Carter from Georgia.

In 1980 President Carter's inability to improve the US economy, and perceived weakness in foreign relations precipitated by the Iranian seizure of US hostages, propelled a Republican resurrection.

Ronald Reagan effortlessly defeated Carter with an overwhelming 489 electoral votes and 51 percent of the popular vote. Additionally, the Republicans won an additional twelve seats in the Senate, taking control of it for the first time in twenty-five years.

This victory was reaffirmed in the 1984 elections when President Reagan won 59 percent of the votes and an overpowering 525 electoral votes, a record at the time; the Republicans lost two Senate seats but retained control of the Senate. However, the Democrats' endeavors did not go unnoticed; they kept control of the House, and in 1986 regained majority status in the Senate.

In 1988 George H. W. Bush won the presidency by a respectably large margin. In 1991, Bush reached a remarkable 89 percent approval rating with his successful recruitment of an international coalition to evict Iranian dictator Saddam Hussein's troops from Kuwait. Inconveniently, domestic issues in the aftermath of the Cold War and public dissatisfaction with persistent government gridlock worked against Bush for his reelection bid against Bill Clinton and the Democrats retained solid majorities in both houses of Congress.

Successfully blocking President Clinton's legislative endeavors, the Republican Party executed an aggressive midterm campaign to gain majority control of both the Senate and the House of Representatives. However, in the 1996 election, Senator Bob Dole lost to Bill Clinton.

In 2000, in what will be known as one of the most contested and controversial elections in US history, the son of ex-president George H. W. Bush won the election by the slimmest of margins. During his first term, President George W. Bush enacted numerous tax cuts, executed preemptive military invasions in Iraq and Afghanistan and, despite his blunders both domestically and internationally, managed to get reelected in 2004. Upon the election of Barack Obama in 2008, Bush left office with the lowest presidential approval ratings ever and a huge national debt; the debt that was growing like a cancerous tumor, along with high unemployment and a banking failure in 2008 that was second only to the Great Depression.

Sources:
http://supreme.lp.findlaw.com/supreme_court/justices/ pastjustices/hughes.html, accessed 3/15/2011.
http://www.history.com/topics/republican-party, accessed 3/15/2011.
http://www.nantucketrtc.org/HistoryoftheRepublicanParty.aspx, accessed 3/15/2011.

CHAPTER 3

HOW SHOULD WE VOTE?

The answer to this question is as varied and diverse as our personalities, backgrounds, and interests, to name a few factors. I, for one, am not defined by any one issue, and my interests cross party lines to go beyond issues that are commonly affiliated with one party or the other. This is why I look at the candidates as individuals, examine their respective views, and look for historical references.

Because of our free elections, there is no right or wrong way of voting as long as we vote with our intellect and not our emotions; as I have often heard, the brain will never understand the matters of the heart. If we use our emotions, we will frequently err in our choices and we will not get the full scope of the issues and how they may affect or benefit us as individuals, in our communities, in our states and, ultimately, in our country. To best answer this question, one must have intrinsic knowledge of our personal needs, values, theories, and philosophies and, above all, be well versed in current events and history.

However, politicians are marketing experts (I will cover that in later chapters), and I assure you that being well informed helps but it will not guarantee that any particular candidate will perform "as advertised," nor will it ensure the right choice. This is where our success as Americans will come in when we unite and make our political representative accountable for their actions, or lack thereof.

We must divorce ourselves from the way we have been doing things and become more eclectic in our approach. I distinctly remember having dinner with my wife and son at a Mexican restaurant in Tallahassee, Florida, and overhearing a conversation from another table where a couple sat with their young son and a friend or relative; this person was telling the couple's son that when he votes all he has to remember was that the *D* in Democrat stood for "dumb"; needless to say, this person was heavily "drinking." Fortunately, the parents were quick to tell their son that the statement was not appropriate and that he should base his decision on facts; kudos to the kid's parents! Regardless, it is certainly an example of someone who is a political supporter without a clue of what would be best for him, let alone our country's overall interest. However, let's not kid ourselves; there are just as many liberals with similar views that are just as detrimental to our overall interest.

You will see in your research that there are many websites that can help you decide how to vote, but be warned: just like any survey the questions or comments can be leading, deceiving, and biased toward the author's own political interests. This is where your analytical aptitude will be challenged; don't take just one survey or examine one source to make your decision. You may also find yourself overwhelmed with volumes of articles, essays, and websites that support and/or refute certain information.

Understanding how policies, legislation, and other factors affect you is the bottom line. Sometimes you will get some interesting perspectives from the most unexpected sources. In fact, I recall having an app on my iPhone on which one of the Internet radio channels was labeled *political comedy*. Needless to say I truly enjoyed it for its entertainment value, but I distinctly remember this one comedian (whose name I can't recall) whose routine was funny and informative. He was saying that there are some people convinced that our current president is part of a conspiracy with the Taliban and other terrorist groups. He went on to mimic a Middle Eastern accent, saying that his plan was to elect a black president—since there have been so many that have been elected in the past—whose name would have to rhyme with Osama's and whose middle name must be the same as that of a ruthless dictator. Now, as funny as it seems you would be surprised at how many oppose president Barack Obama because of his middle name, Hussein, his race, and countless other meaningless attributions that have nothing to do with anything of significance.

Nevertheless, these types of folks are out there, and what is even less fortunate is that regardless of what the facts are, they will not change their views and they will vote based on fallacies and erroneous perspectives. It's easier to just to surround oneself with like-minded contemporaries than to apply intellectual effort and find logical approaches to consider new and different perspectives, even if such perspectives negate or enhance a particular point of view—and at times they can. As long as we keep selecting the path of least resistance when it comes to informing ourselves and we continue to analyze things from a single perspective, things will continue to be stagnant and the world will simply pass us by.

I strongly recommend a book titled *That Used to Be Us: How America Fell Behind in the World It Invented and How We Can Come Back*, by the well-known scholars Thomas L. Freidman and Michael Mandelbaum. Their research and explanations of how things have come to where they are is, to say the least, revealing! Again, it is all part of research and analyzing that we all need to do!

CHAPTER 4

POLITICAL DEBATES AND CAMPAIGNS

I personally do not put much value on all the debates leading to the primary elections. Whatever party is out of the White House will state that everything the president is doing is wrong. Be cognizant of the fact that the platforms of all presidential candidates prior to the primaries are nothing more than marketing presentations; they'll state the obvious and their rhetoric is basically the same. This is evidenced by the fact that once elected all their promises are out the window and it will be politics as usual.

Ultimately, when there are presidential candidates identified after the primaries, that's when they he/she will square off and it is at that time that perhaps some of the real nature of the candidates may be revealed. Regardless, each will still argue about what the outgoing president did or did not do, but it means nothing. We have to look beyond the debate; we need to once again analyze who is funding the campaigns and what special interests are influencing the candidates' agendas. I am just about certain that these special interests do not, for the most part, have our best interests in mind.

How often have we heard that the Republicans are backed by "big business"? Well, I have news for you: "big business" burns the candle at both ends, supporting candidates from either party; it simply hedges its future interests because it will have to buy favors and legislations regardless of who is in power. We, on the other hand, have to grin and bear it, for as long as we allow our elected officials to be bought, we will continue to be culprits in the game. Take a look at Jefferson Williams, the former US senator from Louisiana who is currently serving time in prison for bribery.

Politicians' routines are simple: say what you have to say to get elected or reelected. Once they are elected then it is business as usual, political prostitution, and we end up being the casualty and we are still left with the hot potato. So what are we to do?

The fact of the matter is that the interest of corporations does not always concur with our individual and collective interests. In fact, I find it upsetting that the administration of president Barack Obama released sixty million barrels of federally cached oil to stabilize fuel prices, only to hear that the biggest uproar was from oil companies and other affiliated companies. I think that it's OK for us to occasionally get a break on oil prices. Oil companies have had record-setting profits while many of us struggle to keep roofs over our heads and provide for our families. This is not to detract from oil companies earning record profits; good for them!

For the past few elections, we have heard how cutting taxes helps small businesses decrease unemployment; needless to say, that theory has proven to be false! Let's analyze what has happened since 2000. President George W. Bush provided tax relief for every one of us, but it certainly did not alleviate the unemployment crisis that we faced then. However, he did not instigate the crisis, either, as I am of the opinion that economic trends are cyclical and he happened to be in office when the economy happened to have gone sour. That is not to detract, however, from some of the many blunders that took place during his two terms in office.

Be that as it may, pay close attention to how campaigns manifest themselves. It is during campaigns that we only get half-truths, with excerpts of videos from both sides illustrating what they want us to perceive; I promise you this is not the whole story. What make it even worse are the personal attacks and lies that abound during the campaigns. All the candidates do is analyze what constituents and the news are saying and base their campaign accordingly; again, it's simply *marketing*.

For example, when former senator Tom Daschle wrote creative fiction to the Internal Revenue Service and it became public knowledge in 2009, he withdrew his appointment to head the US Department of Health and Human Services. Thankfully, the Internet and the media made it clear that his supposed innocence was a total farce, and he later apologized; he knew darn well what he had done. Keep in mind, however, that he is not the only one who has done something like this and these acts are totally improper. This is a prime example of how all politicians rely on our ignorance and short-term memory so that they can continue with their political careers. We saw this happen when president Richard Nixon's vice president, Spiro Agnew, was found guilty of tax evasion. I wonder, however, if you and I were to do the same, we simply would not have the resources and inner knowledge of the agencies' directors who may opt to intervene; perhaps.

As if that is not enough, CBS's *60 Minutes* on Sunday November 13, 2011, revealed that many of our congresspersons received "inside trading information" and that this was not illegal until recently. This is a prime example of what we can accomplish: these congresspersons knew that we were fed up with all of them, so they finally passed legislation to ban insider trading information. Nevertheless, the bottom line is that *all politicians are venal; from President Obama to each and every lower politician, regardless of party affiliation or era!*

At the end of the day, we need to do our own research without prejudice and to approach the information we gather without prejudice so that we do not find ourselves being biased by our emotions. Yes, it is easier said than done, but it is also a better approach. It does not matter if you are inclined toward one party or another. You must ask yourself questions—Who? What? Where? Why? When? How?—and finalize your answers by taking into account how the issues affect you, your family, your community, and our country.

If we master the discipline of researching *without prejudice*, I assure you that we will feel better about ourselves and become well-informed voters rather than emotionally motivated voters. The easiest way to motivate ignorance is through fear!

CHAPTER 5

POLLS AND WHAT THEY TELL US

We live in a world of numbers, where computers can digest and process numerical data to tell whatever story we want to tell. Polls are no different; if you have ever taken a statistics course—or "sadistics," as I called it when I was in college—then you know that polls are just another form of statistics that illustrate whatever information the author wants to portray; this is also known as "stratifying" information.

With today's technological advances and polling companies you can find statistics on an array of issues from political to economic studies and everything in between. However, all this data is meaningless if one does not approach it well informed and with multiple sources through which one can do a comparison and contrast on what's being presented.

For example, when President Barack Obama was running for re-election, numerous polls showed that he had a lead on all Republican candidates at the beginning of the Republican primaries. The truth of the matter is that when you group all the Republican candidates at the initiation of the primaries, all the points of the candidates are diluted because the total points are shared; it is, in my humble opinion, useless data. Notice, however, how the margins narrow as prospective candidates drop out of the race until ultimately there is one candidate left after the primaries.

As Election Day approaches, the polls become, to some extent, more accurate as the president and the presidential hopeful begin debating and we start seeing and hopefully understand their positions; still we must view them *with a grain of salt!*

Now, polls, as you can see for yourself, usually have one thousand participants because statistical patterns are usually set with this number. The question, however, is how the information is presented, and that is where the quality of the poll is evident. For example, polls that have "leading questions" like the ones I commonly see with the National Rifle Association's correspondence year in and out are insignificant. They will ask questions for which the best answer is *yes* (or, under certain circumstances, *no*). For example:

☐ Do you believe America needs to be stronger?
☐ Do you feel America is better when Republicans are in office?
☐ Do you believe in the Second Constitutional Amendment?
☐ Do you feel that our government *should have* the right to infringe upon our Second Constitutional Amendment?

Well no kidding Sherlock! Of course the answers will be three consecutive *yeses* and one *no*, but the last question is usually followed with, "If you answered *yes* to one or all of these, then you need to send money!" First, who is the author and what is the purpose? In sales, these are called "qualifying questions," through which a salesperson gauges the prospective client's motivation and interest in being part of a transaction; I sold real estate for the better part of twenty years, and I have been there and done that.

This is not to say that all polls are misleading; Gallup, MSNBC, CNN, HLN, and countless other entities will conduct polls, and as I have mentioned many times, depending on who conducts the poll the outcome may be rather predictable. Once again, it is up to us to practice due diligence by doing our research with a full understanding of where we stand and how issues affect us; remembering this approach will show us that not everything that glitters is gold.

CHAPTER 6

THE DANGERS OF POLITICAL PARTY FANATICISM

Undoubtedly, the subject of politics is, to say the least, passionate. Issues that commonly range from taxes, to personal rights, to entitlements, and even to the size of government are commonly shared by opponents and proponents alike. However, the biggest fault comes in the support of a political party just because it is part of one's culture, regardless of what is said and done, along with justifying whomever we have supported when they are caught doing something wrong.

I have often stated that many people approach politics in the same manner as sports fans do to their favorite team. For example, I am a staunch Miami Dolphins fan; never mind that they have not enjoyed sustained success since the late 1990s, but win, lose, or draw, I will cheer for them and argue tirelessly in their support.

Unfortunately, many staunch Democrats and Republicans do the same; they will criticize the improper behavior from those in the party they oppose, but will excuse it if their candidate exhibits the same improper behavior. It's as if a lower standard is set for the party or persons they support in an effort to excuse—and perhaps even justify—the issue, thus leaving the image of their candidates intact. An example here would be Sarah Palin, who professes moral family values, and yet her daughter became a single mother while still a teenager.

The fact of the matter is that there is no such thing as the "perfect" party or candidate, but with today's technological advances information is so readily available and research can be done effortlessly. Additionally, we must remember what our grade school teachers taught us when we read anything: ask yourself who, why, where, when, and how, and what the interest of the author may be. This may reveal a new perspective, reinforce your current view, change your view or—God forbid—you might learn something new.

What is truly hurtful is that we tend to have a short memory when it comes to facts that define the true character of our political parties and their respective members. That could be why history repeats itself so often: we just do not remember, or choose not to remember. Either way, it is, perhaps, one of our biggest shortcomings.

Moreover, relying on single-source information hinders our ability to analyze the facts. An example of this is listening to just one news source, with a particular political inclination, and assuming that it is the whole truth and nothing but the truth. We also often fail to analyze and study other perspectives that can benefit us by enriching our knowledge and enhancing our ability to analyze things. This is greatly attributed to the fact that politicians appeal to our emotions when campaigning; they tell us what we want to hear and not what we need to know. Yet another example: *all* politicians use fear, fallacies, and hyperbole to gain our support. Don't take my word for it; do a search on Google under "political fallacies" and not only will you get interesting definitions, but you will also find an array of examples from all political angles. In short, politicians rely on our inability to confirm their statements and on our unconditional support; we need to put an end to such reliance!

A good example of this is taxes; politicians scare the daylights out of us with taxes! The Republicans will say that they will cut taxes and that the Democrats will tax us. We hear this every election year; a good example came when Governor Jeb Bush, in his reelection campaign for the Florida gubernatorial race, insisted that Democratic candidate Jim Davis would enact a state income tax. The fact of the matter is that in order for a state income tax to be enacted, it would have to be approved by 75 percent of Florida's voters. Even though Davis profusely contested Governor Bush's erroneous statement and provided the correct information (which could easily have been confirmed with a few keystrokes on any computer with Internet access), many of Bush's proponents continued to repeat the same statement.

I have always said that one can amputate a person's limb, kidnap the children, and have affairs with the spouse, *but don't mess with his or her money*! So politicians will appeal to our emotions and suppress our analytical and intellectual abilities for their own agendas and interests. One example is President George H. W. Bush's (The good Bush) statement, "Read my lips…no new taxes." Yet even though he profusely criticized his predecessor Ronald Reagan's fiscal policies, during Bush's term he passed legislation for new taxes. Ultimately Bush, who I think is one our country's finest presidents, was voted out.

Many support a party because of a single issue; guns, abortion, taxes, and so on. I guess the best way to address this is to say that no one issue defines us as American and, as such, we really need to research as much information as we can to analyze issues with some cognition of how they will affect us as a country and not just rely on one source of information. When doing research you will often find similarities from several sources and that is, more often than not, what confirms validity.

The best example I can think of is how the National Rifle Association (NRA) can, and often does, manipulate information to influence members. I have been a member on and off for the past fifteen years, and I certainly do not agree with all of the group's views. For example, the NRA's *American Hunter* for July 2011 contains an article titled "The Culture War and the Second Amendment." While there is some truth about contemporary culture opposing guns, the NRA claims that gun ownership is down. Clearly that is true in view of the fact at the time we were going through a deep recession bordering on a depression at the time this article was written; so we are all watching our pennies and if I have to choose between paying my living expenses and buying a gun, which is a luxury/hobby, I certainly would make sure that my family was provided for first. However, if I were in the gun industry, I certainly would have been concerned with the slumping sales.

Nevertheless, the NRA, along with countless other organizations that are like-minded, is appealing to the emotions of gun owners; most of these people do not even analyze the content of the article in regards to current economic state. However, that does not detract from the fact that many antigun advocates are ill informed as well and base their opposition on emotions that ultimately are propagated by the news media. Unfortunately we, gun owners, become the casualties for accepting misleading information instead of doing additional research before we make a decision or take a position on any issue.

I guess the most analogous scenario would be, would you sign a contract without reading it and understanding all its terms and conditions blindly? I think the answer is emphatically *no*! But as long as we support our political parties with our emotions, pay attention only to single issues, and suppress our intellectual and analytical abilities, we will undermine the freedoms we have as Americans. In addition, we will continue the spread of unfounded theories and concepts that will ultimately keep us misinformed and ignorant.

CHAPTER 7

POLITICAL PROGRAMS

Do not just rely on radio talk shows and other political programs for information, and certainly do not allow this to be your only source. Many shows, radio and television alike, have their agenda and political affiliations. Take, for example, Rush Limbaugh. Many love him and many hate him, but you have to give him credit because he does his research, he is well informed, and he knows his audience well. While I do not subscribe to his points of view, I occasionally listen to part of his shows. However, more often than not I disagree with his views, but I respect that he does his homework and presents the information to his audience in a comprehensive manner. I have, however, found that there are additional sources to the ones he uses that often do not concur entirely with his views, as well as other sources that entirely refute his statements, but ultimately it's up to me to add to, detract from, reject, or accept what I feel is accurate via proper research. Keep in mind that Limbaugh is not the only one. Piers Morgan is the exact opposite of Rush Limbaugh, and on the occasions that I tune in to Morgan's show, I find myself disagreeing with him as much as I disagree with other extremes.

Countless people hate such shows, and that's fine, but do realize that for what it's worth they are flooding the airways with information that we as Americans should take upon ourselves to analyze before determining what is best for us. The hosts of these shows have their agenda; their points of view are often evident and predictable, and regardless of who is in power, the opponents are going to find areas of disagreement and contention; they will disseminate criticism even on things they once thought were good ideas. The best example of this is former vice president Dick Cheney, who, on national TV, stated that the way in which the administration of President Barack Obama was pursuing Osama Bin Laden was wrong. Well, it took the Obama administration only three years to find and kill Osama bin Laden, while the previous administration of president George W. Bush had been looking for him for seven years to no avail; and I do believe that the Navy Seals and all other military personnel involved had "hunting licenses" to do so—and in the process they did not shoot any of their friends either.

HBO has Bill Maher, who is, in my opinion, more often left of center (though like me he can be either right or left of center, depending on the issue). What I like best is that on his show you can actually see the contrast of the Left and Right. Now, if you ask staunch conservatives about Maher's show they will say people like him, and myself, are just "liberals," or even communists, any way it's sliced. I do not concern myself with what people think about my views and neither should you.

On the other hand, there are others like Anne Coulter whose arguments are emotionally based. Coulter believes that all government employees are parasites who do not contribute in any way, shape, or form to the good of our country. Well, I certainly disagree! If it weren't for government employees, we would not enjoy many of the freedoms we have. Our roads are great, and thank God for our police officers and the military; the list goes on. In fact, any time we hop in an airplane, we know that everything from the construction of the aircraft to its maintenance is highly regulated by the Federal Aviation Administration; isn't air travel one of the safest modes of transportation? Yes, there are those employees who drag their feet, but you will find those in any sector.

One source of information that I have great respect for is Ana Navarro. I find her to be extremely intelligent, and she presents issues in a moderate perspective; her views are truly well balanced, and she will call it as she sees it. She is a Republican, and without any reservation I can say that she is among the best spokespersons the party has to offer along with General Colin Powel. As noted on PRWeb,

> Ana Navarro was born in Nicaragua. In 1980, as a result of the Sandinista revolution, she and her family immigrated to the United States.
>
> Ms. Navarro is a graduate of the University of Miami. In 1993, she obtained her Bachelor in Arts with Majors in Latin American Studies and Political Science. She obtained a Juris Doctorate in 1997. She has expertise on Latin American and Hispanic issues.
>
> She served as the National Co-Chair of Senator John McCain's Hispanic Advisory Council and was a national surrogate for Senator McCain's 2008 presidential campaign. She has played a role in several Federal and State races in Florida. Most recently, she served as National Hispanic Co-Chair for Governor Jon Huntsman's 2012 Campaign. She is a political contributor at CNN and CNN en Español.

In 1997, she was a special advisor to the Government of Nicaragua and in that role; she was one of the primary advocates for NACARA (Nicaraguan Adjustment and Central American Relief Act).

She served on Governor Jeb Bush's transition team and served as his first Director of Immigration Policy in the Executive Office of the Governor. In 1999, Ms. Navarro returned to the private sector and has represented private and public clients on federal issues, particularly related to immigration, trade and policy affecting Central America. In 2001, she served as Ambassador to the United Nation's Human Rights Commission and was a strong advocate for the condemnation of the Government of Cuba for human rights abuses.

Clearly her education and life experience—having to migrate from Nicaragua—gives her a unique perspective, which to some extent is similar to that of many other immigrants who are now living the American Dream. *Good for you, Ana!*

Just as talented and intelligent is Donna Brazile, whose approach is as reasonable and moderate as Navarro's. As noted at Answers.com:

In the fall of 1999, Vice President Al Gore named veteran Democratic Party organizer Donna Brazile as his campaign manager for the 2000 presidential campaign. She became the first African American woman to achieve such a prestigious—and difficult—position in national party politics. Brazile, however, had long been a fixture in Democratic circles, known for her formidable grass-roots organizing skills. In 1987, the

Wall Street Journal named her one of "the powers that (might) be" in national politics in the year 2000. "I'm obsessed with the thought of making things happen.... Ultimately, I do it because I'm scared," confessed Brazile about her career choice to *Washington Post* reporter Donna Britt. "I don't ever, ever, ever want to be poor again. And the best way to insure that won't happen is to organize, to fight for our lives."

Brazile was born in a New Orleans charity hospital on December 15, 1959, and grew up in nearby Kenner, Louisiana. Her father, Lionel, was a Korean War veteran who, at various points in his life, had been run over by a truck, suffered a broken back, and even had a heart attack while riding on a city bus. On that occasion, he simply got off and checked himself into a hospital. There were nine children in the Brazile family, and their father's income as a janitor was not always sufficient, so he often moonlighted or worked double shifts. Brazile's mother also worked as a domestic servant, and the children's grandmother lived with them as well. Brazile used to read the morning paper to her, which helped to foster her interest in politics.

However, we all know who the best political analysts in the world are: each and every one of *us* when we are well informed and intimately cognizant of how policies affect us, our country, and our communities. However, it's human nature to select the path of least resistance, and as long as we choose this path we will never advance as a nation or as individuals, regardless of which administration is in power.

Success lies in comparing and contrasting—in reading diverse sources to get a better perspective.

Sources:

http://www.prweb.com/releases/2013/8/prweb10993443.htm, **accessed on** 11/15/2013.

http://www.answers.com/topic/donna-brazile#ixzz2hzDp8OT1, accessed 11/15/2013.

CHAPTER 8

TAXES

1. We demand our roads to be in great condition for our safety, *but don't tax us for it!*

2. We demand that our airlines be safe, *but don't tax us for it!*

3. We demand that our air traffic controllers be the best trained and have the best equipment money can buy, but don't tax us for it!

4. We demand that our veterans be taken care of with the best medical facilities and staff that money can buy, but don't tax us for it!

5. We demand that our armed forces be the best trained and have cutting-edge technology with which to defend us, but don't tax us for it!

6. We demand that our national security be ahead of the curve against terrorism, but don't tax us for it!

7. We demanded that Saddam Hussein be deposed under the illusion of weapons of mass destruction, but don't tax us for it!

8. We demand that our troops leave the Middle East, but don't tax us for it!

9. We demand to have Social Security available when we retire, but don't tax us for it!

10. We demand that Medicare and Medicaid cover more of our needs, but don't tax us for it!

11. We demand that our police and fire departments have all the equipment and training to assist us when we need them, but don't tax us for it!

12. We demand that our justice system keep felons incarcerated, but don't tax us for it!

13. We demand that our borders be secured, but don't tax us for it!

14. We demand that all illegal immigrants be deported immediately, but don't tax us for it!

15. We demand that the FBI and CIA keep tabs on our enemies with the best technology, training, and personnel, but don't tax us for it!

16. We demand an end to consumer fraud, but don't tax us for it!

17. We demand that our national deficit be paid off, but don't tax us for it!

18. We demand that our national parks be maintained, for us and for future generations, but don't tax us for it!

19. We demand that our wildlife resources be kept healthy, for us and for future generations, but don't tax us for it!

20. We demand that our pharmaceuticals be properly regulated for our health and well-being, but don't tax us for it!

21. We demand that our doctors, nurses, and caregivers have the proper qualifications to help us, but don't tax us for it!

22. We demand that our government help us with stimulus money, grants for education, and grants for starting new business ventures when we are down and out, but don't tax us for it!

23. We demand that unemployment benefits be available if we lose our jobs, *but don't tax us for it!*

24. We demand that emergency services be responsive during natural disasters and national emergencies, *but don't tax us for it!*

25. We demand that our educational system be the best in the world, *but don't tax us for it!*

26. We demand that consumer products be safe for us to use and that their producers and distributors be accountable, *but don't tax us for it!*

27. We demand *freedom, but don't tax us for it!*

We want a lot, and if we are not too careful we might make our country the largest third world country in the universe! I say this as the distance between the rich and the rest of us is widening every day; I have no qualms with the rich, good for them. I do, however, take exception in the way they buy laws and politicians. You and I can't afford that and it puts us in a disadvantage since some of these bought laws that can adversely affect us.

I'm not proponent of tax increases, but I know that small government is the definition of a third world country and excessively large government is the equivalent of communism. Instead of aimlessly going extremely right or left, we should find ways to have "proportionate" government, but how to define that is anyone's guess. Our obligation as Americans is to be well informed and to vote with the foresight our country's forefathers had; we cannot continuously allow our political leaders to exclusively act in their own interests and the interests of those who fund their campaigns, as they have been doing for so many years.

Today we are witnessing a great political change in which the majority of Americans would simply like to tell our leaders in Washington, D.C., "Enough with the political game of partisanship—just get the job done!" This is in fact the very essence of my theory that it has nothing to do with party affiliation but instead addressing the issues in a diligent and concise manner. We cannot in any way, shape, or form expect to have the roads, the military, the police, Social Security, or any of the countless other necessary government services unless they are funded, and the way to fund them is through taxes.

There is no doubt that our government is plagued with careless spending, fraud, and special interests that ultimately we pay for, but that is not to say that we have to continue to allow it. With today's technological advances, how is it possible that our representatives do not devise an electronic voting process on issues in which we would really have a voice? This is just an idea, and there would definitely need to be a "watchdog group" that would ensure that the way our representatives explain issues truly reflects the correct and true nature of the issues themselves so that we can vote accordingly.

If what President Abraham Lincoln so eloquently said in his Gettysburg Address about the government of the people, for the people, and by the people, then why do we not have more say in what is going on in our government? It is our tax money, and we certainly must have a say in how, where, when, and why it is spent. Regardless, our nation's services need to be funded and we need to ensure that we have some leverage over our government representatives beyond voting every two, four, or six years.

It is a fact that the biggest budgetary expenses are in the US Department of Defense, Medicare and Medicaid, and Social Security.

The Defense Department has to be kept in check; research and development for the sort of advanced weaponry that our military and security forces uses is a costly endeavor. For example, let's take a look at the US Air Force's F-22 Raptor, an aircraft that defies all aspects of conventional flight and stealth. This aircraft is so ahead of its time that it can effortlessly dominate the skies over any part of our world; but can it go from door to door checking for terrorists? It is estimated that for every hour the F-22 is flown $50,000 worth of maintenance is required. Furthermore, according to Antiwar.com, each aircraft has a sticker price of just over $350 million! Who benefits from this? The manufacturer does; yes, this manufacturer employs countless people, and yes, the F-22 is a technological marvel, but to date it is my understanding that this awesome aircraft has seen limited combat.

A close friend of mine who is an airline pilot informed that in an effort to promote the F-22 program, information about the F-15 Eagle was withheld in fears that the funding of the F-22 would not be appropriated. Well, I wonder who withheld the information and how? Now, the F-22 is scheduled to replace the "aging" F-15; but the F-15 may not have been so aged after all. This is where a chunk of our taxes go, and this is just a small fraction; we need to have a say on what's being voted for and why!

Our congressional representatives are continuously voting for their own pay raises, while *we* are funding the best pensions known to Americans—and these extend to their spouses too. Whereas I do not object to paying into Social Security, I am making sure that it is not going to be my only source of income when I retire.

However, I know of many people whose only source of retirement income will be Social Security, and it is not a joke as to how financially scant its benefits are. Granted, Social Security was never intended to be anyone's sole income when he or she retires, but why is it that it happens to be the lion share of retirement income for many retired congressional representatives? It's simple: *we have allowed it!*

In the same predicament are Medicare and Medicaid. The truth of the matter is that the medical industry is one of the last cash cows in the United States, and yet for many, these benefits are the only source of health insurance they have. If we were to have taken all the tax money we spent in Iraq looking for "weapons of mass distraction" we could have fully funded health care for every single American and maybe have some left to enhance Social Security!

We have witnessed face-offs between members of Congress and the president regarding "spending caps," and we have to understand where and when this deficit began. Since 2000, the US government has been running a deficit that has ballooned to trillions of dollars mainly because of the cost of military operations in the Middle East and a recession that has ostensibly loosened its grip. However, since both the Democrats and Republicans continue to approach our fiscal issues from political stances, there will never be a comprehensive solution. Party lines need to be erased and collective, commonsense approaches have to be the norm. *Teamwork—what a concept!* However, many of our politicians are more concerned with reelection than with finding common ground on which to address real issues.

I hate to pay taxes as much as anyone else, but how else on God's green earth are we to pay for the national debt? The time to pay the piper has come, and we now have to pay for chasing the illusive weapons of mass destruction—or *distraction*—all over Iraq, as well as the many tax cuts that we have. And yes, those who are worth hundreds of millions, if not billions, should pay a little extra. While it is not fair to tax anyone for their financial success, the reality is that since they can afford to buy legislation and congressional representatives, then I guess it would, perhaps, level the playing field. Corporations like Exxon, HP, IBM, and other conglomerates should also pay their fair share. How often have you heard about the record profits of such giants, yet also hear that their tax contributions are disproportionate to regular individuals like us? Honestly, they seem to tell us, it is not going to affect us common Americans, the 90 percent who comprise the backbone of America!

For example, here is an article I found on the Internet and it states in pertinent part:

Study: 25% of Millionaires Pay Lower Tax Rates than Many Middle-Class Americans

Roughly 25 percent of American millionaires pay a lower tax rate than millions of middle class earners, according to a new study by the nonpartisan Congressional Research Service.

According to the report, which was based on 2006 data, about a quarter of millionaires (about 94,500) paid less than 26.5 percent of their income in federal taxes, while about 10 percent of moderate-income taxpayers (about 10.4 million taxpayers) paid more than 26.5 percent in taxes. …

… billionaire investor Warren Buffett, that the percentage he paid on his taxable income in a given year was "a lower percentage than was paid by any of the other 20 people" in his office. … Washington should raise taxes on the "mega-rich" who have been "coddled long enough by a billionaire-friendly Congress."

Warren Buffet further stateted "no household making over $1 million annually should pay a smaller share of its income in taxes than middle-class families pay."

The study points out that the while, on average, millionaires do pay more in taxes than middle-class earners (about 30 percent compared to about 19 percent), the use of average tax rates in discussions surrounding the issue "hides a great deal of variation in the tax rates that taxpayers actually face."

"The primary reason for this is the higher-income taxpayers with low tax rates receive a very high proportion of the income from long-term capital gains and qualified dividends, which are taxed at low tax rates and not subject to payroll taxes," Hungerford says.

Lower-income taxpayers, however, earn most of their income from wages - which are subject to payroll taxes.

While I would love to continue with more examples of how our tax dollars are being misspent, this book would end up being the largest book ever. The reality is that we have to pay taxes; if most of us are willing to kill or die for our country, why then are we not willing to pay an extra 3 percent in taxes? I guess because (a) it's cheaper to die and (b) our political leaders will misspend it anyway! I'm sure you can come up with a couple of million other reasons too.

Sources:
http://original.antiwar.com/wheeler/2009/03/27/what-does-an-f-22-cost/, accessed 06/22/2010.
http://wiki.answers.com/Q/How_much_does_the_f22_cost, accessed 08/3/2010
Lucy Madison, "Study: 25% of Millionaires Pay Lower Tax Rates Than Many Middle-Class Americans," http://www.wctv.tv/

home/headlines/Study25_of_Millionaires_Pay_Lower_Tax_
Rates_than_Many_Middle-class_Americans_131838728.html,
accessed 08/7/2010.

CHAPTER 9

IT'S OUR OWN FAULT!

Countless times I have heard, that we allow political atrocities due to our short-term memory. Take, for example, William Jefferson, a Democrat; FBI agents found thousands of dollars hidden in his freezer, and ultimately he was found guilty of bribery, yet he was nominated to chair a committee while being investigated! *Why?* Nonetheless, you could find people who supported him, as did some of his Democrat colleagues in a "show of unity." What unity—in *fraud?* Another example is former senator Trent Lott, a Republican from Mississippi, who made comments about how things would have been different if Strom Thurman had been president. While he was asked many times what he meant by that comment, he never answered the question, yet we all know the discriminatory nature of people like Thurmond—and Lott, for that matter. Strom Thurman was a career politician whose career spanned as a state senator in 1932 for the state of South Carolina and became a US Senator in 1954 as a write in candidate. Later in 1956 he ran and won the senate seat. According to www.senated.gov/artandhistory/history/common/ generic/Featured_Bio_Thurmond.htm accessed on 05/18/2014, he held a filibuster against the 1957 Civil Rights act. Furthermore, Strom Thurman's tendencies as evidenced by Toronto Globe and Mail on January 7, 2002 states in pertinent part:

> **He fought school desegregation tooth and claw. In 1957, in an attempt to defeat civil-rights legislation, he embarked on the longest filibuster in Senate history: 24 hours 18 minutes. When Lyndon Johnson nominated Thurgood Marshall as the first black justice of the Supreme Court in 1967, Mr. Thurmond tormented him at the confirmation hearing by asking 60 arcane legal questions.**

This brings to light why would anyone who opposed desegregation and Civil Rights be referenced to how thing should have been? Trent Lott's referencing Strom Thurman's attitude of anti segregation and anti Civil Rights does appear that he agrees with this view.

Fortunately, both Jefferson and Lott have since left office, but I do hope we learned our lessons. Even so, these types of incidents will repeat themselves because we keep reelecting unscrupulous politicians due to our lack of interest in doing research and objectively analyzing facts about the individuals and their actions.

Certainly, these types of corruption are not typical of all Democrats or Republicans, but there is still a lot of corruption in politics. Often when people reach positions of power they tend to let their financial greed and egotism get the best of them. It is then that politicians use their authority and influence to line their pockets and dole out favors to those who generously contribute to their campaigns. All you and I can give, however, is our vote, which is purported the most valuable contribution we have.

I distinctly recall learning in history classes about President Abraham Lincoln's speech on the afternoon of November 19, 1863, at the dedication of the Soldiers' National Cemetery in Gettysburg, Pennsylvania, four and a half months after the Union Army defeated the Confederacy at the decisive Battle of Gettysburg. In the Gettysburg Address Lincoln stated that "this nation shall have a new birth of freedom; and that this government *of the people, by the people, for the* people, shall not perish from the earth" (emphasis added).

This "government *of the people, by the people, for the people*" does not in any way, shape, or form give the authority or latitude for our elected officials to have free reign of the benefits they commonly enjoy—and abuse—when serving in office ostensibly to represent our interests. This is where the recall process is so valuable to us; we need to educate ourselves and insist that all elected officials, excluding those in the federal executive branch, be subject to recall; at present, only state officials may be recalled. Right now in Florida, where I live, we have a situation in which current governor Rick Scott is leading Florida to a non democratic state, where the state government is not of the people, is not by the people, and certainly is not for the people. His attempt to institute mandatory drug testing of all state employees is, at very least, a conflict of interest because his wife's company (formerly his own company) happens to perform such specimen analysis.

Why is it that politicians insist on higher standards that they themselves do not adhere to? Because of our short-term memory, our inability to look beyond what is being offered and/or presented, and our willingness to accept things at face value. Education is by far the most powerful tool we have, and I assure you that, beyond high school, all accredited institutions will require research; it's that simple!

The worst part is how politicians insist on "accountability" and "transparency." But isn't it funny how we only hear these terms during election years? I have yet to think of any campaign speech that does not include such terms. That being said, why did Hillary Clinton state during her bid for the Democratic presidential nomination in 2008 that she remembered dodging bullets when she arrived in Bosnia in the fall of 1996? I urge you to go to YouTube, type in "Hillary Clinton in Bosnia," and select the ABC News video. What truly amazes me is that in that video an individual states that she was referring to "other" firing. *Yeah, right!* Now, I do not want to only single out a Democrat. Let's talk about our forty-third president, George W. Bush. I voted against him three times, in the 2000 primary and in the 2000 and 2004 general elections. One of the few good things that came out of his administration is that finally Dan Quail was surpassed in the ability to make inarticulate public speeches. It absolutely baffles me as to how someone so inarticulate was voted in as president, and I am truly not surprised that history now shows him to be the least popular president. When you search for "Bushisms" on the Internet the amount of data that comes up is astonishing. Do the same search yourself if you doubt me, and look for video examples on YouTube.

For example, as noted on the Democracy Now website, "When President Bush was questioned about tribal sovereignty in the 21st century at a gathering of minority journalists he responded: 'Tribal sovereignty means that. It's sovereign. You're a…you're a…you've been given sovereignty and you're viewed as a sovereign entity.'"

Yet, some even argue that Bush was one of the best presidents ever! I was appalled when I went to a gun show and saw some vendors selling T-shirts with an image of him winking and a caption that read, "Miss me yet?" Yes, I miss him like I miss a root canal without Novocain, or like I miss an ingrown toenail.

Bush stated early in his first term that the federal government's budget surplus was *our* money, and he pushed to reimburse all of us with that surplus. My question now is, if that surplus belonged to us, then who does our current deficit belong to? Logically, just as we received such "reimbursement" then, shouldn't we now pay our fair share to get our country back on track financially?

President Bush is now out of office and we have Barack Obama as president, who is currently serving his last term. Mark my words, Republican candidates are simply going to sling mud at anything the Democrats have done, as if to imply that they have better answers to the nation's problems. Of all possible future candidates for the 2016 elections, I do not see any who is worth my vote at this time for either party. If we as Americans expect our voices to be heard, without political party lines, we just might have a chance to truly steer our country in a better, more equitable direction. Until then, my friends, we are just going to repeat history and dig ourselves deeper into the hole we find ourselves in now. My good friend, the airline pilot, said it best: "Every election, it seems that all we do is pick our poison."

Sources:

http://www.realclearpolitics.com/lists/most_corrupt_politicians/
	dwyer.html, accessed 10/13/2010

http://www.democracynow.org/2004/8/10/bush_on_native_
	american_issues_tribal, accessed 8/11/2011

CHAPTER 10

STATE GOVERNMENT

For over eleven years I have had the privilege and honor to work for the State of Florida. I started in December 1998, just as governor Jeb Bush was elected, and I have to say it has been an eye-opening experience. I elected to join the ranks of state government because my real estate career's income was, to say the least, a wild roller coaster ride, and with a baby on the way I needed affordable health insurance, a steady income, and a pension plan for my family's financial future.

Prior to joining the state government ranks, I had the same view of government employees as Ann Coulter and many other staunch conservatives had which was that all civil servants were unworthy of any compensation or merits. Additionally, former governor Bob Martinez had stigmatized Florida state employees with his remarks that government employees were "lard bricks."

I am proud to inform you that our government is just as competent—and as incompetent—as the private sector. As I mentioned in chapter 9, governor Rick Scott is steering Florida toward becoming the first state in the Union not to strive for an appropriate economic development; it is ironic that an individual who resigned as Chief Executive of Columbia/HCA in 1997 amid a controversy over the company's business and Medicare billing practices; the company ultimately admitted to fourteen felonies and agreed to pay the federal government over $600 million, which was the largest fraud settlement in US history, is now the governor of Florida.

Several law suits have been filed against Scott for actions that seem to breach contractual obligations and/or Florida law since he took office; that's nothing new as just about all governors have been sued. One of the lawsuits filed was because Governor Scott passed legislation requiring that all welfare recipients undergo a drug test and if any individual was tested positive for drug use, they are to pay for the cost of the test. Well, wouldn't you know that only 2 percent or less tested positive for drug use? As a result, *we the tax payers* are footing the bill! Oh, and it just so happens that his wife is the head of a specimen-testing company. Thank God that Governor Scott has the taxpayers' interest in mind—imagine what it would be like if he didn't! What are the chances that those who are on welfare can afford drugs, or will pay the penalties even if they test positive? Let's see—aren't most people who are on welfare ethnic minorities? I guess he has it in for those who are poor and nonwhite.

Additionally, Scott's crass ignorance of government is axiomatic; he likes to run a dictatorship in which he operates as it's "my way or the highway;" well Rick, I hate to break the news to you, but there is a reason we have constitutions, laws, and administrative rules; to keep people like you from running a government of personal interest.

While I am not proud of my disparagement of Rick Scott, I can't help but voice my disapproval, as he does not have Florida's best interests in mind. He also said that he is going to bring accountability to state government; gee, where have we heard that before?

Since Governor Scott believes in accountability for government, he should pay out of his own pocket for all the welfare drug tests that come out negative; now *that* is accountability. Yet, if you were to have the opportunity to ask him about this failure he would either not answer you or give you a roundabout answer that would not address the question and quickly move on to something else. I have seen him do this in person and I frankly fear his ignorance and self-serving interests.

Additionally, Governor Scott wants to reduce regulations for business; is that not what the administration of President George W. Bush did with the Mineral Management Services (MMS)? We ended up with a massive oil spill in the Gulf of Mexico. Without regulations, how are business and their respective officers going to be held accountable? Yet, many staunch conservatives, libertarians, and Tea Party supporters think that small to no government is ideal; imagine what people with wealth like many of our politicians would be capable of with their own interests in the bottom line. Isn't that why, during the Industrial Revolution, regulations evolved—to stop the abuse of natural and human resources and look out for those who did not have the means to preserve them?

As I have recently learned in the book *Foundations of Financial Management*, it was deregulation that got us into the recent recession—the longest recession since the Great Depression. With deregulation of financial institutions and the unwillingness to enforce risk-management controls, loans were being made to countless entities that not only did not qualify for the loans and never had the intention of paying back these loans. Additionally, the ease with which money was lent, and with inadequate credit screening, allowed for financial "engineers" to create portfolios of mortgage-backed securities that included these high-risk loans. Consequently, Congress is now working on new regulations for financial institutions that will hopefully prevent this from happening again.

As it is, large corporations do not pay their fair share of taxes as compared to the vast majority of citizens—and I include those who write creative fiction to the Internal Revenue Service every year! There is plenty of data on hand for you to read, analyze, and draw your own conclusions from as you see fit; be sure to do your research!

What really angers me is the comparison to the private sector, as if it was to be the standard against which all things should be measured; the fact of the matter is that government cannot and should not operate like the private sector, where everything is for a bottom-line profit. Government's bottom line should be how it serves the people by supporting infrastructure and aiding in economic growth, and this should take place with unbiased agendas. But that only happens in utopia. This is not to say that government should have its hands in everything; I will reiterate what I said earlier: I don't believe in either overly small or overly large government; the challenge is finding the proper balance; and I assure you that governor Rick Scott and others like him have no interest in seeking a proper balance. Now, clearly the reason I picked Governor Scott is due to the fact that I live in Florida. I should point out that *I did not vote for him on either elections*!

Among Florida's finest governors were Charlie Crist, Lawton Chiles, and Bob Graham. Florida prospered under their leadership and yes the fact that the US economy was booming did help, but I can assure you that under Bob Martinez, Jeb Bush, and Rick Scott that is when the party ended.

Governor Charlie Crist was governor as a Republican and this past midterm election he ran as a Democratic gubernatorial candidate, which he regrettably lost. This is the essence of my argument, regardless Governor Charlie Crist is still Florida's best choice regardless of what party he is affiliated with. He proved when he was in office his stellar ways as a Republican Governor and I assure that he would have done a great job if given the chance. I would even go as far to say that he would be an ideal President given the opportunity because he is a moderate and above all he really relates well to most, if not all, Americans.

Governor Jeb Bush initiated privatization of certain government operations that to this day have yet to prove financially beneficial for Florida. It did, however, enhanced Bush's relations with those who took advantage of the privatization, like one aerospace company that was awarded the service of vocational rehabilitation; in some instances the company abandoned the program and left the state holding the hot potato.

It was during this period that we began to witness a rise in unemployment. I do not think this can be blamed entirely on Jeb Bush's administration, because economic trends tend to be cyclical, but Jeb Bush's policies did not help the situation. Florida had enough revenue generated to sustain core services, yet Jeb Bush cut taxes left and right; the average Floridian did not reap any rewards, but those in the upper income echelons certainly did. Consequently, state government services are being slashed that actually afforded the vast majority of Floridians and tourists to enjoy many of the beauties of the great state of Florida.

The private sector is not the answer for all problems for reasons already mentioned. We need a government in which it is not the elite calling the shots. Once again I quote Abraham Lincoln's Gettysburg Address: "this nation shall have a new birth of freedom; and that this government *of the people, by the people, for the people,* shall not perish from the earth" (emphasis added).

While I am not advocating that the homeless should lead the nation, we have certainly seen what the elite are capable of; we need compassion and reasonability, and once again the goal should be to identify the challenges we are faced with. While no one has all the right answers, when we participate by voting in every election, and do so from a well-informed stance, that so-called illusive challenge becomes more attainable and will provide us, and our country, with a sense of direction. In order for us to ensure that we have a say, regardless of political affiliation, we need to become informed at all levels of politics, all the way up to our highest office, the White House.

Just stop and think: when you get in your car and drive several hundred miles on our highways cruising at seventy miles per hour (or in my case faster than that, as I have been known to have been "awarded" citations for land speed records), do you ever worry about your safety? The roads in the United States are among the best in the world, law enforcement is readily available (in my case particularly when I don't need it), and information is also available. Who do you think takes care of this, and does a good job of it? Our government!

How about when we climb in a large, state-of-the art jet airplane; who do you think mandates maintenance, qualification, and standards? Our government, of course! Why, then, do we not give credit where credit is due? If you think that a private company would do better, then look at how and who runs third world countries. I assure you that you will see that although our government may not be perfect, it provides us with the best roads, emergency services, and law enforcement, as well as countless other services that we all take for granted. Now, I will admit that some agencies are ruthless, like the Internal Revenue Service, which ensures that you pay Uncle Sam what they think you owe, yet the United States has the highest level of compliance in the world when it comes to taxes.

All this starts at the smallest political subdivisions, such as town council member and mayor, and it progresses up to the national ranks, but the real issue is having our political leaders understand how their policies affect the average American. This is why I have such a gripe with leaders like Bill Clinton, George W. Bush, Jeb Bush, and Rick Scott, who do not have a clue how you and I struggle to make ends meet, while others, by their own accounts, have made it "from rags to riches."

I'll tell you this much: if I were Florida's governor, a US congressman, or even the president, the first thing I'd do would be to pass a constitutional amendment that would allow recall and mandate for any and all elected officials so that they are personally liable for any legislation they compose or endorse should it not prove to be beneficial to the operation of the government and for the majority of the American people. This, of course, would be in a ballot, and I am sure that it would pass! This might help reduce governmental fraud and—oh my—that is true accountability! If it hadn't been for the support of my wife and son, in addition to working for the State of Florida, my associate degree in arts education would have been vastly expensive. With the grants available, earning my bachelor's was just as tough. But I took advantage of those grants, and of federal loans, and earned my bachelor's degree nonetheless from Flagler College in Tallahassee, Florida, in May 2011.

Let's not forget the 3 percent pay cut for all Florida state employees that Governor Scott approved, because in the private sector it is common practice that employees pay into their pensions. Well, Governor Scott, Florida state employees are the lowest paid in the United States, have the fewest per capita in the United States, and costs of living is outpacing earnings; and now you slam state employees with a 3 percent pay cut? This is evident that when certain people find their way into positions of authority, they do not see how their actions adversely affect the lives of so many; they lose touch with the realities of the common folk like us. As it is, my wife and I are barely making ends meet; this is one reason why I earned a bachelor's degree, but it has not yet begun to pay back. There are countless other people in the same boat, but many of our leaders do not care.

So the next time you travel within your state, or out of your state, remember that the safety, convenience, and privilege of good roads, safe airlines, and protection from the world's best military are being accomplished with government employees paid by our tax dollars.

As Dale Carnegie commented in his book *How to Win Friends and Influence People*, "Any fool can criticize—and most fools do." Do not be so sure that our government is so incompetent; look at companies like Enron. Governor Rick Scott himself was part of Federal investigation. As was noted in the *Miami Herald*,

> "...federal investigators found that Scott took part in business practices at Columbia/HCA that were later found to be illegal—specifically, that Scott and other executives offered financial incentives to doctors in exchange for patient referrals, in violation of federal law, according to lawsuits the Justice Department filed against the company in 2001.
>
> The doctor payments were among 10 different kinds of fraud identified by the Justice Department in its 10-year probe of the company, records show. Three years after Scott left Columbia/HCA, the company admitted wrongdoing, pleading guilty to 14 felonies—most committed during Scott's tenure—in addition to paying two sets of fines totaling $1.7 billion...."

And yet he was elected and reelected!

Sources:

Stanley B. Block, Geoffrey A. Hirt, and Bartley F. Danielsen, "Risk Management and the Financial Crisis," in *Foundations of Financial Management*, 14th ed. (New York: McGraw-Hill, 2010), 6–7.

Beth Reinhard, "Rick Scott's Role in Columbia/HCA scandal," *Miami Herald*, June 27, 2010, http://miamiherald.typepad.com/nakedpolitics/2010/06/rick-scotts-role-in-columbiahca-scandal.html#ixzz1ZsfnkbRy, accessed **07/08/2013**.

http://www.examiner.com/article/did-you-know-gov-rick-scott-used-his-company-to-perform-mandatory-drug-tests accessed on 08/22/2014

CHAPTER 11

SOCIAL SECURITY

Here is Wikipedia's information on Social Security, as accessed on **02/17/2013**:

> Social Security is a social insurance program that is funded through payroll taxes called Federal Insurance Contributions Act tax (FICA). Tax deposits are formally entrusted to the Federal Old-Age and Survivors Insurance Trust Fund, the Federal Disability Insurance Trust Fund, the Federal Hospital Insurance Trust Fund, or the Federal Supplementary Medical Insurance Trust Fund.
>
> The main part of the program is sometimes abbreviated and referred to [as] OASDI (Old Age, Survivors, and Disability Insurance) or RSDI (Retirement, Survivors, and Disability Insurance). When initially signed

into law by President Franklin D. Roosevelt in 1935 as part of his New Deal, the term Social Security covered unemployment insurance as well. The term is used to refer only to the benefits for retirement, disability, survivorship, and death, which are the four main benefits provided by traditional private-sector pension plans. In 2004 the U.S. Social Security system paid out almost $500 billion in benefits.

By dollars paid, the U.S. Social Security program is the largest government program in the world and the single greatest expenditure in the federal budget, with 20.8% for social security, compared to 20.5% for discretionary defense and 20.1% for Medicare/Medicaid.[6] Social Security is currently the largest social insurance program in the U.S. where in 2003 combined spending for all social insurance programs constituted 37% of government expenditure and 7% of the gross domestic product. Social Security is currently estimated to keep roughly 40 percent of all Americans age 65 or older out of poverty. The Social Security Administration is headquartered in Woodlawn, Maryland, just to the west of Baltimore.

The 2011 annual report by the program's Board of Trustees noted the following: in 2010, 54 million people were receiving Social Security benefits, while 157 million people were paying into the fund; of those receiving benefits, 44 million were receiving retirement benefits and 10 million disability benefits. In 2011, there will be 56 million beneficiaries and 158 million workers paying in. In 2010, total income was $781.1 billion and expenditures were $712.5 billion, which meant a total net increase in assets of $68.6 billion. Assets in 2010 were $2.6 trillion, an amount that is expected to be adequate to cover the next 10 years. In 2023, total income and interest earned on assets are projected to no longer cover expenditures for Social Security, as demographic shifts burden the system. By 2035, the ratio of potential retirees to working age persons will be 37 percent—there will be less than three potential income earners for every retiree in the population. The trust fund would then be exhausted by 2036 without legislative action.

Proposals to privatize Social Security recently became part of the Social Security debate during the Bill Clinton and George W. Bush presidencies.

It never ceases to amaze me how many people are against Social Security, yet many people would not have any income whatsoever in their senior years if it were not for Social Security. Let's not forget, that Medicare and Medicaid play a huge part in all this; yet because their political party opposes these programs, their supporters do too notwithstanding the fact they need the benefits themselves.

While I do not recall when and where, I remember seeing media coverage of a town hall meeting regarding the Affordable Care Act (aka "Obama care") in which the moderator asked members of the audience, "Who is collecting Social Security and participating in either Medicare or Medicaid?" A substantial portion of the audience members raised their hands. This question was followed up with, "Those who support Obama care, put your hands down. Now, those who oppose Obama care, are you willing to relinquish Medicare or Medicaid?" Then all those who opposed Obama Care lowered their hands; the audience was composed of both Republicans and Democrats.

Let's face it: if we do not start protesting about how corporate America influences our political policies, we are going to end up back in the era before the Industrial Revolution, when the workforce was simply treated like livestock. Even to get a decent pension from any employer today is a miracle, and most of us do not save enough to see us through our retirement! Florida's governor Rick Scott, and many like him, are so removed from the common folk that they are ignorant to the realities of how we make ends meet. Their wealth has made them "recession-proof." In Florida, state employees are now forced to pay 3 percent of their salaries into an already funded pension, and for any employee who averages $24,000 a year that is a huge impact.

Governor Scott justifies this because in the private sector there are no pension plans to speak of; therefore, why should the State of Florida have one? Well, it's simple: because it will keep countless people from having to file for welfare and other social aide that would ultimately cost everyone. Additionally, since the pay is meager, pensions are one of the few reasons why people work for the government to begin with.

The cost of living is rising, the cost of health care has become prohibitively expensive, and yet there are those who, if it wasn't for these very social programs, would have even less than they have now. "Obama Care" has been torn to pieces by those who do not need assistance with health insurance, like our senators, congressman, and corporate America.

That is why we are seeing the protests that are being organized: we need to stop corporate America from running this country for their sole benefit and to our detriment. Most of our political representatives only care about how much they can collect for their campaigns and what favors they can do while in office, only to cash in on them when they are out of office, if they are going to wait that long. Yet, who can we ask to help us when we need social services?

What really irks me is when people say that for those who are not rich, or are unemployed it is due to their own fault. Give me a break!

Please, show me someone who voluntarily chose not to be well off or unemployed! For what it's worth, there are those who simply believe what iconic figures say and do not even try to see how it affects them. *This is why you need to be intimately informed of how policies affect you!*

For as long as we remain indifferent about our political issues, we may end up losing programs like Social Security, Medicare, and Medicaid. I am not advocating that you solely rely on these programs, but the reality of this is that many who oppose these programs could use these programs. As I have mentioned earlier, I personally know of some people whose only income is that of Social Security and if it weren't for Medicare and Medicaid they would not have any services or income, yet they oppose the Affordable Care Act and the very social services they need and receive. Go figure! Additionally, Social Security was never designed to be anyone's sole source of income, instead its design is as a supplement to whatever pension or retirement income you may have set up or earned during your professional working life.

Unless you earn six-digit salaries and are extremely frugal, chances are you will not save enough money for your retirement. In the United States, the status quo is what many strive to achieve, and that is part of the reason why many families ended up having their homes foreclosed upon. If they cannot afford to buy the car, they'll lease it. If they cannot afford the down payment on a house, they'll take two mortgages. And while they live from paycheck to paycheck they will criticize the government's social programs, for which they are only a paycheck away from qualifying for.

So now I ask you, is Social Security worth saving and paying into? I think so; and should we have a better health care system? You bet we should!

Source:
"Social Security (United States)," Wikipedia, Http://en.wikipedia. org/wiki/Social_Security_(United_States)#cite_note-www.ssa. gov.650-4, accessed 03/05/2012.

CHAPTER 12

DIVERSE TOPICS

Perhaps the most argued aspects of politics are the personal issues such as religion, sexual orientation, moral beliefs, and personal character, to name a few. I feel that some, if not most, of these topics have no place in politics.

For example, how often have you heard the condemnation of homosexuality or bisexuality because the Bible addresses it? All I have to say about homosexuality, bisexuality, and even asexuality is that if God is the creator of everything that is seen and unseen, then who are we to judge any of God's creations? I believe in God and Jesus, and I believe that since *we* are all God's children I doubt that he would disown any of us because of how he made us. If one of your children is gay, would you disown him or her? Would it change his or her being? If you can answer yes to either of these questions, I have news for you: you will still be that child's mother or father—for eternity. Certainly, God would not disown him or her because, as I see it, the only unforgivable sin is not believing in God.

Furthermore, one of the greatest things about our country is the separation of church and State. Analyze countries that govern in the name of God and compare their standards and quality of life. More people have died in the name of God than any other reason known to humankind such as the "Holy wars?" Let's stop the hypocrisy and see things for what they are. We have developed politics where the most common practice is disseminating statements directed toward political opponents; this is clearly not congruent with God's way of "love thy neighbor."

The best analogy I can think of is if two people are in a car accident they are both are devout Christians and they are both killed, would God not receive either of them because if his or her sexual orientation when one is gay and the other is a pedophile? Would God choose? I think that at this time is best to let the subject rest....

Let's take a look at former president Bill Clinton. While I do not think he is the best president in recent history, he did happen to have been president during a great economic growth cycle. But he did inappropriately interacted with and had an affair with an intern who clearly planned it and he played into her hand. But, President Clinton, not thinking like a responsible person, fell right into Monica Lewinsky's plan; she never cleaned the dress that she wore when this incident took place? Hmmm... Yes, it was wrong, but all President Clinton should have said was that it was nobody else's business. The only difference between President Clinton and countless others is that he was caught.

On a sarcastic note, rumor has it that many are concerned that if Hillary Clinton becomes president, that former President Bill Clinton will have some influence on her while being president. Well, rumor has it that Hillary will have him run a cigar shop in the cafeteria of the White House, but what Hillary does not know is that Bill has proposed to Monica Lewinsky to offer humidor services in this cigar shop. LOL!!! I can just imagine the play Saturday Night Live would make of this.

Firearms

Another topic that is a pet peeve of mine is the gun issue. I am a proud member of the National Rifle Association and my local gun club, and it irks me when the vast majority of gun opponents refuse to see the facts. Granted, that is not to say that some of their points are not valid, but a total ban of firearms in the United States is not the answer! They want to ban guns because they are used to kill and to commit crimes; then let's ban any and all artifacts that have killed people or aided in the commission of crimes.

Many even think that only assault rifles are for killing people. Well, I have news for you: 9/11 proved that with a box cutter you can control an entire aircraft! But let's not stop there. How many people have died in alcohol-related deaths? The difference is that the government collects copious amounts of tax revenue from alcohol, but I do not see anyone complaining besides the alcohol manufacturers.

Additionally, I feel compelled to explain the different types of firearms since there is an evident misconception regarding assault rifles. First and foremost, unless you are licensed by the federal government you *cannot* simply buy a fully automatic weapon. A semiautomatic firearm is one that after you pull the trigger once, you have to release it and press it again to fire it as its mechanism will load another round in the chamber.

Regarding high-capacity magazines, please understand that these magazines are so prolific that banning them would only raise their price as countless gun owners have them; some in unreasonable quantities. The fact of the matter is that Hollywood and the media have repressed common sense, and many opponents of firearms do not bother with doing a little research. I assure you that if you go to any gun store, let them know that you do not know much about firearms, and ask for information. They will gladly tell you all that you need to know regarding safety, the proper use of firearms and laws.

While I am not a "trophy deer hunter," I absolutely love the outdoors, and hunting has become a tradition in my family for many years. In fact, there are other sports, such as those of the United States Pistol Shooter's Association (USPSA), that allow participants to safely enjoy fast-action shooting. Do yourself a favor and go to the USPSA's website (http://www.uspsa.com) and watch the video that explains the events; then, if that does not interest you, that's fine. But because you do not agree or because you hate firearms that does not mean that everyone else should share your views, or be restricted of enjoying such sports. At least now you have done a little research and know a little more.

Indubitably, the most plausible explanation of crimes committed with firearms has been noted by family psychologist John Rosemond of Gastonia, North Carolina, who in a column for the *State*, the newspaper of Columbia, South Carolina, stated in part that

> "..gun issues are not symptomatic of lax gun control, but rather lax parents, lax schools, lax discipline, lax standards, lax expectations, and a culture which has become lax to the point of virtual indifference when it comes to morals, personal responsibility, and critical thinking."

While I support his statement, I also feel that too many parents take the path of least resistance and hope that schools and other institutions, along with other public entities, will show their children the things that the parents themselves should be teaching them. The worst excuse is that juveniles at risk learn illicit behavior through TV, movies, and the Internet; my question to these parents is where they when their children were "learning" illicit behavior through these media? While there are some exceptions based on socioeconomic and family predicaments, countless children who were brought up in broken homes and in less than ideal communities have become well-respected citizens.

Without a doubt, the mass shootings that take place are tragedies. But stop and analyze this: we are a country of how many millions of people and, according to the Federal Bureau of Investigations, there are over two hundred million guns in private hands in the United States. Crunch the numbers and you'll see that these tragic events are *statistically* insignificant. Just ask any statistician and he or she will tell you that these regrettable tragedies are outliers. More people die of smoking, drinking, car accidents and other causes than of gun incidents. Granted, if you or any relative or friend is a casualty, that is 100 percent awful, but these events are the exception and do not in any way, shape, or form represent the 99.98 percent of gun owners in America. That is not to say, however, that there are people that can't spell "gun" and have one too many guns, but nevertheless this issue needs to be put in perspective. I highly encourage you to do your research, and I am certain that you will see that the gun issue is hyperbole on the part of the media, whose tenet is simple: "If it bleeds, it leads."

Gambling

While I do not gamble, my take on it is simple: if you do not agree with it then don't gamble. Gambling does generate jobs, and countless people enjoy it. And, like the sale of alcohol, it provides revenue to our government system, from which, directly or indirectly, *we all benefit.*

Immigration

I do not fault those who seek a better life here in the United States, but we need to do something about the immigration issue. I just do not understand why the federal government doesn't offer amnesty in exchange for evidence leading to employers of illegal immigrants. I think that would make employers think twice before hiring illegal immigrants and also clean the slate by severely punishing those who have employed illegal immigrants with fines and jail time in addition to confiscation of assets. As I understand it, all they have to show is a social security card and social security cards do not have pictures; hmmm, I wonder what is wrong with this?

The immigration problem is not new; in fact I recall that it was an issue during the administration of President Ronald Reagan, and clearly it is still today. Therefore neither the administrations of Ronald Reagan, George H. W. Bush, Bill Clinton, George W. Bush, nor Barack Obama have resolved this issue. Something needs to be done, but what exactly I certainly do not know. I will say that many of the illegal immigrants are good people seeking a good life and efforts should be made to mitigate this issue.

Drugs

Many argue that the legalization and taxation of drugs may be the answer to the drug problem n the United States. Frankly, I do not know, nor do I subscribe to this point of view. I fear that legalization might open the floodgates of drug use, thus requiring policing from all levels of government, and this might cost more than what it may procure in taxes. I simply do not know what the best answer might be. But if we all do our homework and inform ourselves, we just might be better-informed voters and be part of the solution.

The Electoral College

The Electoral College, which comprises selected electors designed to elect the president, is one college that we could forgo! For the most part, these electors represent different organizations that are representative of interests and thus vote in a particular way; they do not, alas, always represent the general wishes of the population. For example, Bill Clinton won his first term as president due solely to actions of the Electoral College, not the popular vote. So did George W. Bush's first term.

The reason I say that we could forgo this institution is that as history has shown, the Electoral College does not always concur with our collective interest—the popular vote. So, the question is, do our votes really count? As mentioned above, the college is composed of those who represent particular interests. Well, then, what is the use of us voting at all if members of the Electoral College are curtailed to vote a particular way?

Reportedly, this system is part of a mechanism where there is complex districting like we have in this country. I do not believe in the Electoral College. Let the people chose, and not a handful of selected elites! The popular vote alone is what should decide who becomes president.

CHAPTER 13

LET'S TALLY THE SCANDAL SCORE

I Googled "political scandals in the United States" and the most comprehensive article was that of Wikipedia; I am fully cognizant that this source is publicly edited, but I hope that it will motivate you to research it for yourself and that it will lead you to other areas you have never heard or seen before. Cross-referencing the names of the individual politicians via Internet searches proved that the article is indeed accurate. This article spans from the 1789–1796 administrations of President George Washington to 2009 and the administration of President Barack Obama. One fact is clear: the political party affiliated with whatever administration is in power seems to lead the scandals at that time.

Nevertheless, it illustrates that both Democrats and Republicans are as corrupt as they come. Thus is the reason why I quoted Mark

Twain at the opening of this book: "It could probably be shown by facts and figures that there is no distinctly Native American criminal class except Congress."

On website Wikipedia.com you will find the article "List of Federal Political Scandals in the United States," which is reproduced in its entirety below with the exception of the deletion of certain bracketed text and endnote references and some slight changes in formatting; all content remains intact.

List of Federal Political Scandals in the United States
This article provides a list of political scandals of the United States, sorted from most recent date to least recent.

Scope and organization of political scandals
The article is organized by presidential terms and then divided into scandals of the Executive, Legislative and Judicial Branches. Members of both parties are listed under the term of the president in office at the time the scandal took place.

Scandals: There is no hard and fast rule defining scandals. Scandal is defined as "loss of or damage to reputation caused by actual or apparent violation of morality or propriety." In politics scandal should be kept separate from 'controversy,' (which implies two differing points of view) and 'unpopularity.' Many decisions are controversial, many decisions are unpopular—that alone does not make them scandals.

A good guideline is whether or not an action is, or appears to be, illegal. Since everyone, particularly a politician, is expected to be law abiding, breaking the law is, by definition, a scandal. Misunderstandings, breaches of ethics, unproven crimes or cover-ups may or may not result in scandals depending on who is bringing the charges, the amount of publicity garnered, and the seriousness of the crime, if any. The finding of a court with jurisdiction is the sole method used to determine a violation of law.

There is no bright line to distinguish "major" scandals from "minor" scandals, but rather scandals tend to be defined by the public themselves and the media's desire to feed that particular frenzy. Thus, small but salacious scandals, such as Larry Craig's (R-ID) arrest for lewd behavior can eclipse more serious scandals such as suspending the Writ of Habeas Corpus in time of war.

What is also unclear is how far down the ladder of obscurity a scandal should go. During the Truman (D) administration, 196 local IRS staffers were found to be corrupt, but they were so far removed from Washington, Truman or any of his appointees, that it could hardly be called a 'Truman scandal.'

Also not included in this article are pervasive systemic scandals, such as the role of money in "normal" politics which purchases access and influence. Neither are 'revolving door' stories, which is the practice of hiring government officials to promote or lobby for companies they were recently paid to regulate. Though some rules now apply, to a great extent this is legal in the United States.

Politicians are those who make their living primarily in politics, their staffs and appointees. By definition, political scandals should involve politicians and not private citizens. Private Citizens should be included only when they are closely linked to elected or appointed politicians such as party officials. Kenneth Lay of Enron is a good example of such a citizen. This list also does not include crimes which occur outside the politician's tenure unless they specifically stem from acts while they were in office.

Scope: To keep the article a manageable size, Senators and Congressmen who are rebuked, admonished, condemned, suspended, found in contempt, found to have acted improperly, used poor judgment or were reprimanded by Congress are not included unless the scandal is exceptional or leads to expulsion.

Federal government scandals
2009– Obama Administration

Legislative Branch

☐ John Ensign (R-NV) the religious conservative resigned his Senate seat on May 3, 2011 before the Senate Ethics Committee could examine possible fiscal violations in connection with his extramarital affair with Cynthia Hampton. (2011).

☐ Charles B. Rangel (D-NY) Rangel was found guilty on 11 charges by the House Ethics Committee. On December 2, 2010, the full House of Representatives voted 333-79 to censure Rangel. (2010)

☐ Tom DeLay (R-TX) On November 24, 2010 a Texas jury convicted DeLay of money laundering connected to the Jack Abramoff scandal. (2010) On January 10, 2011, he was sentenced to three years in prison in Texas.

☐ Joe Wilson (R-SC) The congressman from Carolina interrupted a major televised speech about health care reform by President Barack Obama to a joint session of Congress. After Obama said that no illegal aliens would be accepted under his health plan, Rep. Wilson shouted, "You lie!" The incident resulted in a formal rebuke by the House of Representatives. He later admitted that the outburst was "inappropriate." (2009)

Judicial Branch

☐ G. Thomas Porteous The Federal Judge for Eastern Louisiana was unanimously impeached by the US House of Representatives on charges of corruption and perjury in March 2010. He was convicted by the US Senate and removed from office. He had been appointed by Bill Clinton. (2010)

☐ Samuel B. Kent The Federal District Judge of Galveston, Texas was sentenced to 33 months in prison for lying about sexually harassing two female employees. He had been appointed to office by George H. W. Bush in 1990. (2009)

2001–2008 George W. Bush Administration
Executive Branch

☐ Lewis Libby (R) Chief of Staff to Vice President Dick Cheney (R), 'Scooter' was convicted of perjury and obstruction of justice in the Plame Affair on March 6, 2007. He was sentenced to 30 months in prison and fined $250,000. The sentence was commuted by George W. Bush (R) on July 1, 2007. The felony remains on Libby's record though the jail time and fine were commuted.

☐ Alphonso Jackson (R) The Secretary of Housing and Urban Development resigned while under investigation by the FBI for revoking the contract of a vendor who told Jackson he did not like President George W. Bush (R). (2008)

☐ Karl Rove (R) Senior Adviser to President George W. Bush was investigated by the Office of Special Counsel for "improper political influence over government decision-making," as well as for his involvement in several other scandals such as Lawyergate, Bush White House e-mail controversy and Plame affair. He resigned in April 2007.

☐ "Lawyergate" Or the Dismissal of U.S. attorneys controversy refers to President Bush firing, without explanation, eleven Republican federal prosecutors whom he himself had appointed. It is alleged they were fired for prosecuting Republicans and not prosecuting Democrats. When Congressional hearings were called, a number of senior Justice Department officials cited executive privilege and refused to testify under oath and instead resigned, including:

1. Michael A. Battle (R) Director of Executive Office of US Attorneys in the Justice Department

2. Bradley Schlozman (R) Director of Executive Office of US Attorneys who replaced Battle

3. Michael Elston (R) Chief of Staff to Deputy Attorney General Paul McNulty

4. Paul McNulty (R) Deputy Attorney General to William Mercer

5. William W. Mercer (R) Associate Attorney General to Alberto Gonzales

6. Kyle Sampson (R) Chief of Staff to Attorney General Alberto Gonzales

7. Alberto Gonzales (R) Attorney General of the United States

8. Monica Goodling (R) Liaison between President Bush and the Justice Department

9. Joshua Bolten (R) Deputy Chief of Staff to President Bush was found in Contempt of Congress

10. Sara M. Taylor (R) Aid to Presidential Advisor Karl Rove

11. Karl Rove (R) Advisor to President Bush

12. Harriet Miers (R) Legal Counsel to President Bush, was found in Contempt of Congress

☐ Bush White House e-mail controversy—During the Lawyergate investigation it was discovered that the Bush administration used Republican National Committee (RNC) web servers for millions of emails which were then destroyed, lost or deleted in possible violation of the Presidential Records Act and the Hatch Act. George W. Bush, Dick Cheney, Karl Rove, Andrew Card, Sara Taylor and Scott Jennings all used RNC webservers for the majority of their emails. Of 88 officials, no emails at all were discovered for 51 of them. As many as 5 million e-mails requested by Congressional investigators of other Bush administration scandals were therefore unavailable, lost, or deleted.

☐ Lurita Alexis Doan (R) Resigned as head of the General Services Administration. She was under scrutiny for conflict of interest and violations of the Hatch Act. Among other things she asked GSA employees how they could "help Republican candidates."

☐ Jack Abramoff Scandal in which the prominent lobbyist with close ties to Republican administration officials and legislators offered bribes as part of his lobbying efforts. Abramoff was sentenced to 4 years in prison.

1. David Safavian GSA (General Services Administration) Chief of Staff, found guilty of blocking justice and lying, and sentenced to 18 months.

2. Roger Stillwell (R) Staff in the Department of the Interior under George W. Bush. Pleaded guilty and received two years suspended sentence.

3. Susan B. Ralston (R) Special Assistant to the President and Senior Advisor to Karl Rove, resigned October 6, 2006 after it became known that she accepted gifts and passed information to her former boss Jack Abramoff.

4. J. Steven Griles (R) former Deputy to the Secretary of the Interior pleaded guilty to obstruction of justice and was sentenced to 10 months.

5. Italia Federici (R) staff to the Secretary of Interior, and President of the Council of Republicans for Environmental Advocacy, pled guilty

to tax evasion and obstruction of justice. She was sentenced to four years probation.

6. Jared Carpenter (R) Vice-President of the Council of Republicans for Environmental Advocacy, was discovered during the Abramoff investigation and pled guilty to income tax evasion. He got 45 days, plus 4 years probation.

7. Mark Zachares (R) staff in the Department of Labor, bribed by Abramoff, guilty of conspiracy to defraud.

8. Robert E. Coughlin (R) Deputy Chief of Staff, Criminal Division of the Justice Department pleaded guilty to conflict of interest after accepting bribes from Jack Abramoff. (2008)

☐ Kyle Foggo Executive director of the CIA was convicted of honest services fraud in the awarding of a government contract and sentenced to 37 months in federal prison at Pine Knot, Kentucky. On September 29, 2008, Foggo pleaded guilty to one count of the indictment, admitting that while he was the CIA executive director, he acted to steer a CIA contract to the firm of his lifelong friend, Brent R. Wilkes.

☐ Julie MacDonald (R) Deputy Assistant Secretary of the Department of the Interior, resigned May 1, 2007 after giving government documents to developers. (2007)

☐ Claude Allen (R) Appointed as an advisor by President Bush on Domestic Policy, Allen was arrested for a series of felony thefts in retail stores. He was convicted on one count and resigned soon after.

☐ Lester Crawford (R) Commissioner of the Food and Drug Administration, resigned after 2 months. Pled guilty to conflict of interest and received 3 years suspended sentence and fined $90,000. (2006)

☐ 2003 Invasion of Iraq depended on intelligence that Saddam Hussein was developing "weapons of mass destruction" (WMDs) meaning nuclear, chemical and/or biological weapons for offensive use. The Downing Street memo were minutes of a British secret meeting with the US (dated 23 July 2002, leaked 2005) which include a summary of MI6 Director Sir Richard Dearlove's report that "Bush wanted to remove Saddam, through military action, justified by the conjunction of terrorism and WMD. But the intelligence and the facts were being fixed around the policy" This was called the 'smoking gun' concerning W. Bush's run up to war with Iraq. (2005)

☐ Yellowcake forgery: Just prior to the 2003 invasion of Iraq, the Bush administration presented evidence to the UN that Iraq was seeking material (yellowcake uranium) in Africa for making nuclear weapons. Though presented as true, it was later found to be not only dubious, but outright false.

☐ Coalition Provisional Authority Cash Payment Scandal; On June 20, 2005 the staff of the Committee on Government Reform prepared a report for Congressman Henry Waxman. It was revealed that $12 billion in cash had been delivered to Iraq by C-130 planes, on shrink wrapped pallets of US $100 bills. The United States House Committee on Oversight and Government Reform, concluded that "Many of the funds appear to have been lost to corruption and waste....

Some of the funds could have enriched both criminals and insurgents...." Henry Waxman, commented, "Who in their right mind would send 363 tons of cash into a war zone?" A single flight to Iraq on December 12, 2003 which contained $1.5 billion in cash is said to be the largest single Federal Reserve payout in US history according to Henry Waxman.

☐ Bush administration payment of columnists with federal funds to say nice things about Republican policies. Illegal payments were made to journalists Armstrong Williams (R), Maggie Gallagher (R) and Michael McManus (R) (2004–2005)

☐ Sandy Berger (D) former Clinton security adviser pleads guilty to a misdemeanor charge of unlawfully removing classified documents from the National Archives in 2005.

☐ Bernard Kerik (R) nomination in 2004 as Secretary of Homeland Security was derailed by past employment of an illegal alien as a nanny, and other improprieties. On Nov 4, 2009, he pled guilty to two counts of tax fraud and five counts of lying to the federal government and was sentenced to four years in prison.

☐ Torture: Top US officials including George W. Bush and Dick Cheney authorized enhanced interrogation techniques of prisoners, including waterboarding (called torture by many) by US troops and the CIA in Iraq, Afghanistan, and elsewhere. In 2010 Bush stated "He'd do it again..." and Cheney stated on ABC's This Week, "I was a big supporter of waterboarding." (2004)

☐ Plame affair (2004), in which CIA agent Valerie

Plame's name was leaked by Richard Armitage, Deputy Secretary of State, to the press in retaliation for her husband's criticism of the reports used by George W. Bush to legitimize the Iraq war.

☐ Thomas A. Scully, (R) administrator of the Centers for Medicare and Medicaid Services (CMS), withheld information from Congress about the projected cost of the Medicare Prescription Drug, Improvement, and Modernization Act, and allegedly threatened to fire Medicare's chief actuary, Richard Foster, if Foster provided the data to Congress. (2003) Scully resigned on December 16, 2003.

☐ NSA warrantless surveillance—Shortly after the September 11 attacks in 2001, President George W. Bush (R) implemented a secret program by the National Security Agency to eavesdrop on domestic telephone calls by American citizens without warrants, thus by-passing the FISA court which must approve all such actions. (2002) In 2010, Federal Judge Vaughn Walker ruled this practice to be illegal.

☐ Kenneth Lay (R) a member of the Republican National Committee, financial donor and ally of George W. Bush and once considered a possible Secretary of the Treasury. Lay was found guilty of 10 counts of securities fraud concerning his company Enron, but died before sentencing.

☐ Janet Rehnquist (R) appointed Inspector General of the Department of Health and Human Services by George W. Bush. In 2002, Governor Jeb Bush's (R-FL) Chief of Staff Kathleen Shanahan asked Rehnquist to delay auditing a $571 million federal overpayment to the State of Florida. Rehnquist ordered her staff to delay the investigation for five months until after the Florida elections. When Congress began an investigation in to the matter, Rehnquist resigned in March 2003, saying she wanted to spend more time with her family.

☐ John Yoo (R) An attorney in the Office of Legal Counsel inside the Justice Department who, working closely with vice president Dick Cheney and The Bush Six, wrote memos stating the right of the president to—

1. suspend sections of the ABM Treaty without informing Congress]bypass the Foreign Intelligence Surveillance Act allowing warrentless wiretapping of US Citizens within the United States by the National Security Agency.

2. state that the First Amendment and Fourth Amendments and the Takings Clause do not apply to the president in time of war as defined in the USA PATRIOT Act.

3. allow Enhanced Interrogation Techniques (torture) because provisions of the War Crimes Act, the Third Geneva Convention, and the Torture convention do not apply.

Many of his memos have since been repudiated and reversed. Later review by the Justice Department reported that Yoo and Jay Bybee used "poor judgement" in the memos, but no charges have yet been filed.

Legislative Branch

☐ Ted Stevens Senator (R-AK) convicted on seven counts of bribery and tax evasion October 27, 2008 just prior to the election. He continued his run for re-election, but lost. Once the Republican was defeated in his reelection, new US Attorney General Eric Holder (D) dismissed the charges "in the interest of justice" stating that the Justice Department had illegally withheld evidence from defense counsel.

☐ Charles Rangel (D-NY) failed to report $75,000 income from the rental of his villa in Punta Cana, Dominican Republic and was forced to pay $11,000 in back taxes. (September 2008)

☐ Rick Renzi (R-AZ) Announced he would not seek another term. Seven months later, on February 22, 2008 he pleaded not guilty to 35 charges of fraud, conspiracy and money laundering.

☐ Jack Abramoff Scandal, (R) lobbyist found guilty of conspiracy, tax evasion and corruption of public officials in three different courts in a wide ranging investigation. Currently serving 70 months and fined $24.7 million.... The following were also implicated:

1. Tom DeLay (R-TX) The House Majority Leader was reprimanded twice by the House Ethics Committee and his aides indicted (2004–2005); eventually DeLay himself was investigated in October 2005 in connection with the Abramoff scandal, but not indicted. DeLay resigned from the House 9 June 2006. Delay was found to have illegally channeled funds from Americans for a Republican Majority to Republican state legislator campaigns. He was convicted of two counts of money laundering and conspiracy in 2010.

2. Michael Scanlon (R) former staff to Tom DeLay: working for Abramoff, pled guilty to bribery.

3. Tony Rudy (R) former staff to Tom DeLay, pleaded guilty to conspiracy.

4. James W. Ellis (R) executive director of Tom DeLay's political action committee, Americans for a Republican Majority (ARMPAC), was indicted by Texas for money laundering.

5. John Colyandro (R) executive director of Tom DeLay's political action committee, Texans for a Republican Majority (TRMPAC), was indicted by Texas for money laundering.

6. Bob Ney (R-OH) pleaded guilty to conspiracy and making false statements as a result of his receiving trips from Abramoff in exchange for legislative favors. Ney received 30 months in prison.

7. Neil Volz (R) former staff to Robert Ney, pleaded guilty to one count of conspiracy in 2006 charges stemming from his work for Bob Ney. In 2007 he was sentenced to two years probation, 100 hours community service, and a fine of $2,000.

8. William Heaton (R), former chief of staff for Bob Ney (R), pleaded guilty to a federal conspiracy charge involving a golf trip to Scotland, expensive meals, and tickets to sporting

events between 2002 and 2004 as payoffs for helping Abramoff's clients.

9. John Albaugh (R) former chief of staff to Ernest Istook (R-OK) pled guilty to accepting bribes connected to the Federal Highway Bill. Istook was not charged. (2008)

10. James Hirni, (R) former staff to Tim Hutchinson (R-AR) was charged with wire fraud for giving a staffer for Don Young (R) of Alaska a bribe in exchange for amendments to the Federal Highway Bill. (2008)

11. Kevin A. Ring (R) former staff to John Doolittle (R-CA) was convicted of five charges of corruption.

☐ John Doolittle (R-CA) both he and his wife were under investigation (January 2008). Under this cloud, Doolittle decided not to run for reelection in November 2008. The Justice Department announced in June 2010 they had terminated the investigation and found no wrong doing.

☐ Randy Cunningham (R-CA) pleaded guilty on November 28, 2005 to charges of conspiracy to commit bribery, mail fraud, wire fraud and tax evasion in what came to be called the Cunningham scandal. Sentenced to over eight years.

☐ Kyle Foggo Executive director of the CIA was convicted of honest services fraud in the awarding of a government contract and sentenced to 37 months in the federal prison at Pine Knot, Kentucky. On September 29, 2008, Foggo pleaded guilty to one count of the indictment, admitting that while CIA executive director he acted to steer a CIA contract to the firm of his lifelong friend, Brent R. Wilkes.

☐ Cynthia McKinney (D-GA) struck a U.S. Capitol Police officer in the chest after he attempted to stop her from going around a security checkpoint. McKinney apologized on the floor of the House and no charges were filed. (March 29, 2006)

☐ William J. Jefferson (D-LA) in August 2005 the FBI seized $90,000 in cash from Jefferson's home freezer. He was re-elected anyway, but lost in 2008. Jefferson was convicted of 11 counts of bribery and sentenced to 13 years on November 13, 2009, and his chief of staff Brett Pfeffer was sentenced to 84 months in a related case.

☐ Bill Janklow (R-SD) convicted of second-degree manslaughter for running a stop sign and killing a motorcyclist. Resigned from the House and given 100 days in the county jail and three years. (2003)

☐ Robert Torricelli Senator (D-NJ) after 14 years in the House and one term in the Senate, Torricelli declined to run again when accused of taking illegal contributions from Korean businessman David Chang. (2002)

☐ Jim Traficant (D-OH) found guilty on 10 felony counts of financial corruption, he was sentenced to 8 years in prison and expelled from the House. (2002)

1993–2000 Bill Clinton Administration
Executive Branch

☐ Webster Hubbell (D) Associate Attorney General, pleaded guilty to mail fraud and tax evasion while in private practice.[109] Sentenced to 21 months in prison. (1995)

☐ Henry Cisneros (D) Secretary of Housing. Resigned and plead guilty (1999) to a misdemeanor charge of lying to the FBI about the amount of money he paid his former mistress, Linda Medlar while he was Mayor of San Antonio, Texas. He was fined $10,000. (1999)

☐ Ronald Blackley (D) Secretary of Agriculture Mike Espy's Chief of Staff, sentenced to 27 months for perjury. Mike Espy was found innocent on all counts. http://laws.findlaw.com/dc/983036a.html. (1999)

☐ Bill Clinton President (D) Impeached for perjury and obstruction of justice for allegedly lying under oath about sexual relations with intern Monica Lewinsky. Clinton was acquitted by the Senate and remained in office. Clinton subsequently was cited for contempt of court and agreed to a five-year suspension of his Arkansas law license. (1998). On October 1, 2001, Bill Clinton was barred from practicing law before the Supreme Court of the United States. (2001)

☐ Pardongate President Bill Clinton (D) granted 140 pardons on his last day in office January 20, 2001 for a total of 396. which seemed large compared to the total of 74 by George H. W. Bush, but not when compared to Ronald Reagan's total of 393.

☐ Whitewater scandal (1994–2000) independent counsel Kenneth Starr (R) investigated the Clintons' role in peddling influence for the Whitewater (real estate) Development Corporation while he was Governor of Arkansas. No criminal charges were brought against either President Bill Clinton (D) or First Lady

Hillary Clinton. (D)

☐ Wampumgate Bruce Babbitt (D), Secretary of the Interior 1993–2001, accused of lying to Congress about influencing a 1995 American Indian tribe casino decision. Babbitt was cleared of all wrongdoing.

☐ Filegate alleged misuse of FBI resources by Clinton Security Chief, Craig Livingstone (D), to compile an 'enemies' list (1996); Investigation found insufficient evidence of criminal wrongdoing.

☐ Vincent Foster (D) the White House lawyer was alleged to have been murdered by either Bill or Hillary Clinton, for various reasons and with varying degrees of involvement. The suicide was investigated by the Park Police Service, the FBI, Independent Consultant Robert Fiske and finally by Independent Counsel Kenneth Starr all of whom ruled that it was a simple suicide. (1993)

☐ Travelgate, involving the firing of White House travel agents. In 1998 Independent Counsel Kenneth Starr (R) exonerated President Bill Clinton and Hillary Clinton of any involvement. (1993)

Legislative Branch

☐ Barbara-Rose Collins (D-MI) found to have committed 11 violations of law and house rules stemming from use of campaign funds for personal use.

☐ Wes Cooley (R-OR), Cooley was convicted of having lied on the 1994 voter information pamphlet about his service in the Army. He was fined and sentenced to two years probation. (1997)

☐ Austin Murphy (D-PA) convicted of engaging in voter fraud for filling out absentee ballots for members of a nursing home.

☐ Newt Gingrich (R-GA), the Speaker of the House, was accused of financial improprieties leading to House reprimand and $300,000 in sanctions leading to his resignation. (1997)

☐ Walter R. Tucker III (D-CA) resigned from the House before conviction on charges of extortion and income tax fraud while he was Mayor of Compton, California. Sentenced to 27 months in prison. (1996)

☐ Nicholas Mavroules (D-MA) pleaded guilty to bribery charges.

☐ House banking scandal The House of Representatives Bank found that 450 members had overdrawn their checking accounts, but had not been penalized. Six were convicted of charges, most only tangentially related to the House Bank itself. Twenty-two more of the most prolific over-drafters were singled out by the House Ethics Committee. (1992)

1. Buzz Lukens (R-OH) convicted of bribery and conspiracy.

2. Carl C. Perkins (D-KY) pled guilty to a check kiting scheme involving several financial institutions (including the House Bank).

3. Carroll Hubbard (D-KY) convicted of illegally funneling money to his wife's 1992 campaign to succeed him in congress.

4. Mary Rose Oakar (D-OH) was charged with seven felonies, but pleaded guilty only to a misdemeanor campaign finance charge not related to the House Bank.

5. Walter Fauntroy (D-DC) convicted of filing false disclosure forms in order to hide unauthorized income.

6. Jack Russ Sgt. at Arms, convicted of three counts.

7. Congressional Post Office scandal (1991–1995) A conspiracy to embezzle House Post Office money through stamps and postal vouchers to congressmen.

8. Dan Rostenkowski (D-IL) Rostenkowski was convicted and sentenced to 18 months in prison, in 1995.

9. Joe Kolter (D-PA) Convicted of one count of conspiracy[134] and sentenced to 6 months in prison.

10. Robert V. Rota Postmaster, convicted of one count of conspiracy and two counts of embezzlement.

☐ Jay Kim (R-CA) accepted $250,000 in illegal 1992 campaign contributions and was sentenced to two months house arrest. (1992)

1989–1992 George H. W. Bush Administration
Executive Branch

☐ George H. W. Bush (R) President. During his election campaign, Bush denied any knowledge of the Iran Contra Affair by saying he was "out of the loop." But his own diaries of that time stated "I'm one of the few people that know fully the details..." He repeatedly refused to disclose this to investigators and won the election. (1988)

☐ Catalina Vasquez Villalpando, (R) Treasurer of the United States. Pleaded guilty to obstruction of justice and tax evasion. The only US Treasurer ever sent to prison. (1992)

☐ Iran-Contra Affair pardons. On December 24, 1992, George H. W. Bush (R) granted clemency to five convicted government officials and Caspar Weinberger, whose trial had not yet begun. This action prevented any further investigation into the affair.

1. Caspar Weinberger (R) Secretary of Defense under Ronald Reagan

2. Robert C. McFarlane (R) National Security Advisor to Ronald Reagan

3. Elliott Abrams Asssistant Secretary of State to Ronald Reagan

4. Clair George CIA Chief of Covert Ops

5. Alan D. Fiers Chief of the CIA's Central American Task Force

6. Duane Clarridge (R) CIA Operations Officer

Legislative Branch

☐ Albert Bustamante (D-TX) convicted of accepting bribes.

☐ Lawrence J. Smith (D-FL) pleaded guilty to tax fraud and lying to federal election officials and served three months in jail, fined $5,000, 2 years probation and back taxes of $40,000.

☐ David Durenberger Senator (R-MN) denounced by Senate for unethical financial transactions and then disbarred (1990). He pled guilty to misuse of public funds and given one year probation. (1995)

Judicial Branch

☐ Clarence Thomas (R) Supreme Court nominee accused of sexual harassment by former employee Anita Hill. He was approved anyway.

☐ Walter Nixon US Judge (D-MS) Was impeached by the House and convicted by the Senate for perjury on November 3, 1989.

1981–1988 Ronald Reagan Administration

Executive Branch

☐ Raymond J. Donovan (R) Secretary of Labor under Ronald Reagan, was investigated and acquitted of larceny and fraud concerning subway construction in New York City. (1987)

☐ Housing and Urban Development Scandal A scandal concerning bribery by selected contractors for low income housing projects.

1. Samuel Pierce (R) Secretary of Housing and Urban Development because he made "full and public written acceptance of responsibility" was not charged.

2. James G. Watt (R) Secretary of Interior, 1981–1983, charged with 25 counts of perjury and obstruction of justice, sentenced to five years probation, fined $5,000 and 500 hours of community service.

3. Deborah Gore Dean (R) Executive Assistant to (Samuel Pierce, Secretary of HUD 1981–1987, and not charged). Dean was convicted of 12 counts of perjury, conspiracy, bribery. Sentenced to 21 months in prison. (1987)

4. Phillip D. Winn (R) Assistant Secretary of HUD, 1981–1982, pled guilty to bribery in 1994.

5. Thomas Demery, (R) Assistant Secretary of HUD, pled guilty to bribery and obstruction.

6. Joseph A. Strauss, (R) Special Assistant to the Secretary of HUD, convicted of accepting payments to favor Puerto Rican land developers in receiving HUD funding.

7. Silvio D. DeBartolomeis convicted of perjury and bribery.

☐ Wedtech scandal Wedtech Corporation convicted of bribery for Defense Department contracts:

1. Edwin Meese (R) Attorney General, resigned but never convicted.

2. Lyn Nofziger (R) White House Press Secretary, whose conviction of lobbying was overturned.

3. Mario Biaggi (D-NY) sentenced to 2-1/2 years.

4. Robert García (D-NY) sentenced to 2-1/2 years.

☐ Savings and loan scandal in which 747 institutions failed and had to be rescued with $160,000,000,000 of taxpayer monies in connection with the Keating Five.

☐ Iran–Contra Affair (1985–1986); A plan conceived by CIA head William Casey (R) and Oliver North (R) of the National Security Council to sell TOW missiles to Iran for the return of US hostages and then use part of the money received to fund Contra rebels trying to overthrow the left wing government of Nicaragua, which was in direct violation of Congress' Boland Amendment. Ronald Reagan appeared on TV stating there was no "arms for hostages" deal, but was later forced to admit, also on TV, that yes, there indeed had been:

1. Caspar Weinberger (R) Secretary of Defense, was indicted on two counts of perjury and one count of obstruction of justice on June 16, 1992. Weinberger received a pardon from George H. W. Bush on December 24, 1992 before he was tried.

2. William Casey (R) Head of the CIA. Thought to have conceived the plan, was stricken ill hours before he would testify. Reporter Bob Woodward records that Casey knew of and approved the plan.

3. Robert C. McFarlane (R) National Security Adviser, convicted of withholding evidence, but after a plea bargain was given only 2 years probation. Later pardoned by President George H. W. Bush.

4. Elliott Abrams (R) Asst Sec of State, convicted of withholding evidence, but after a plea bargain was given only 2 years probation.

Later pardoned by President George H. W. Bush. http://www.fas.org/irp/offdocs/walsh/summpros.htm.

5. Alan D. Fiers Chief of the CIA's Central American Task Force, convicted of withholding evidence and sentenced to one year probation. Later pardoned by President George H. W. Bush.

6. Clair George Chief of Covert Ops-CIA, convicted on 2 charges of perjury, but pardoned by President George H. W. Bush before sentencing.

7. Oliver North (R) convicted of accepting an illegal gratuity, obstruction of a congressional inquiry, and destruction of documents, but the ruling was overturned since he had been granted immunity.

8. Fawn Hall, Oliver North's secretary was given immunity from prosecution on charges of conspiracy and destroying documents in exchange for her testimony.

9. John Poindexter National Security Advisor (R) convicted of 5 counts of conspiracy, obstruction of justice, perjury, defrauding the government, and the alteration and destruction of evidence. The Supreme Court overturned this ruling.

10. Duane Clarridge An ex-CIA senior official, he was indicted in November 1991 on 7 counts of perjury and false statements relat-

ing to a November 1985 shipment to Iran. Pardoned before trial by President George H. W. Bush.

11. Richard V. Secord Ex-major general in the Air Force who organized the Iran arms sales and Contra aid. He pleaded guilty in November 1989 to making false statements to Congress. Sentenced to two years of probation.

12. Albert Hakim A businessman, he pleaded guilty in November 1989 to supplementing the salary of North by buying a $13,800 fence for North with money from "the Enterprise," which was a set of foreign companies Hakim used in Iran-Contra. In addition, Swiss company Lake Resources Inc., used for storing money from arms sales to Iran to give to the Contras, pled guilty to stealing government property. Hakim was given two years of probation and a $5,000 fine, while Lake Resources Inc. was ordered to dissolve.

13. Thomas G. Clines Once an intelligence official who became an arms dealer, he was convicted in September 1990 on four income tax counts, including underreporting of income to the IRS and lying about not having foreign accounts. Sentenced to 16 months of prison and fined $40,000.

14. Carl R. Channell A fund-raiser for conservative causes, he pleaded guilty in April 1987 to de-

frauding the IRS via a tax-exempt organization to fund the Contras. Sentenced to two years probation.

15. Richard R. Miller Associate to Carl R. Channell, he pleaded guilty in May 1987 to defrauding the IRS via a tax-exempt organization led by Channell. More precisely, he pled guilty to lying to the IRS about the deductibility of donations to the organization. Some of the donations were used to fund the Contras. Sentenced to two years of probation and 120 of community service.

16. Joseph F. Fernandez CIA Station Chief of Costa Rica. Indicted on five counts in 1988. The case was dismissed when Attorney General Dick Thornburgh refused to declassify information needed for his defense in 1990.

☐ Inslaw Affair (1985–1994+); a protracted legal case that alleged that top-level officials of President Ronald Reagan's (R) Department of Justice were involved in software piracy of the Promis program from Inslaw Inc. forcing it into bankruptcy. Attorney General Edwin Meese (R) and his successor Attorney General Dick Thornburgh (R) were both found to have blocked the investigation of the matter. They were succeeded by Attorney General William P. Barr (R) who also refused to investigate and no charges were ever filed.

1. D. Lowell Jensen, (R) Deputy Attorney General was held in Contempt of Congress.

2. C. Madison Brewer A high ranking Justice Department official was held in Contempt of Congress.

☐ Michael Deaver (R) Deputy Chief of Staff to Ronald Reagan 1981–85, pleaded guilty to perjury related to lobbying activities and was sentenced to 3 years probation and fined $100,000.

☐ Sewergate A scandal in which funds from the EPA were selectively used for projects which would aid politicians friendly to the Reagan administration.

1. Anne Gorsuch Burford (R) Head of the EPA. Cut the EPA staff by 22% and refused to turn over documents to Congress citing "Executive Privilege," whereupon she was found in Contempt and resigned with twenty of her top employees. (1980)

2. Rita Lavelle (R) An EPA Administrator, U.S. Environmental Protection Agency misused 'superfund' monies and was convicted of perjury. She served six months in prison, was fined $10,000 and given five yrs probation.

Legislative Branch

☐ David Durenberger Senator (R-MN), denounced by the Senate for unethical financial transactions (1990) and then disbarred as an attorney. In 1995 he pled guilty to 5 misdemeanor counts of misuse of public funds and was given one years probation.

☐ Jesse Helms Senator (R-NC), His campaign was found guilty of "voter caging" when 125,000 postcards were sent to mainly black neighborhoods and the results used to challenge their residency and therefore their right to vote. (1990)

☐ Barney Frank Congressman (D-MA), Lived with convicted felon Steve Gobie who ran a gay prostitution operation from Frank's apartment without his knowledge. Frank was Admonished by Congress for using his congressional privilege to eliminate 33 parking tickets attributed to Gobie. (1987)

☐ Donald E. "Buz" Lukens (R-OH), Convicted of two counts of bribery and conspiracy. (1996)

☐ Anthony Lee Coelho (D-CA) Resigns rather than face inquiries from both the Justice Department and the House Ethics Committee about an allegedly unethical "junk bond" deal, which netted him $6,000. He was never charged with any crime. (1989)

☐ Jim Wright (D-TX) House Speaker, resigned after an ethics investigation led by Newt Gingrich alleged improper receipt of $145,000 in gifts. (1989)

☐ Keating Five (1980–1989) The failure of Lincoln Savings and Loan led to Charles Keating (R) donating to the campaigns of five Senators for help. Keating served 42 months in prison. The five were investigated by the Senate Ethics Committee which found that:

1. Alan Cranston Senator (D-CA) reprimanded

2. Dennis DeConcini Senator (D-AZ) acted improperly

3. Don Riegle Senator (D-MI) acted improperly

4. John Glenn Senator (D-OH) used poor judgment

5. John McCain Senator (R-AZ) used poor judgment

☐ Abscam FBI sting involving fake 'Arabs' trying to bribe 31 congressmen. (1980) The following [seven] Congressmen were convicted:

1. Harrison A. Williams Senator (D-NJ) Convicted on 9 counts of bribery and conspiracy. Sentenced to 3 years in prison.

2. John Jenrette Representative (D-SC) sentenced to two years in prison for bribery and conspiracy.

3. Richard Kelly (R-FL) Accepted $25K and then claimed he was conducting his own investigation into corruption. Served 13 months.

4. Raymond Lederer (D-PA) "I can give you me" he said after accepting $50K. Sentenced to 3 years.

5. Michael Myers (D-PA) Accepted $50K saying, "…money talks and bullshit walks." Sentenced to 3 years and was expelled from the House.

6. Frank Thompson (D-NJ) Sentenced to 3 years.

7. John M. Murphy (D-NY) Served 20 months of a 3-year sentence.

8. Also arrested were NJ State Senator Angelo Errichetti (D)and members of the Philadelphia City Council.

☐ Mario Biaggi (D-NY), Convicted of obstruction of justice and accepting illegal gratuities he was sentenced to 2½ years in prison and fined $500K for his role in the Wedtech scandal, see above. Just before expulsion from the House, he resigned. The next year he was convicted of another 15 counts of obstruction and bribery. (1988)

☐ Pat Swindall (R-GA) convicted of 6 counts of perjury. (1989)

☐ George V. Hansen (R-ID) censured for failing to file out disclosure forms. Spent 15 months in prison.

☐ James Traficant (D-OH), convicted of ten felony counts including bribery, racketeering and tax evasion and sentenced to 8 years in prison. He was expelled from the House July 24, (2002.)

☐ Frederick W. Richmond (D-NY), Convicted of tax evasion and possession of marijuana. Served 9 months. (1982)

☐ Dan Flood (D-PA) censured for bribery. After a trial ended in a deadlocked jury, pleaded guilty and was sentenced to a year's probation.

☐ Joshua Eilberg (D-PA) pleaded guilty to conflict-of-interest charges. In addition, he convinced president Carter to fire the U.S. Attorney investigating his case.

Judicial Branch

☐ Alcee Hastings (D-FL), Federal District court judge impeached by the House and convicted by the Senate of soliciting a bribe (1989). Subsequently elected to the U.S. House of Representatives. (1992)

☐ Harry Claiborne (D-NE), Federal District court Judge impeached by the House and convicted by the Senate on two counts of tax evasion. He served over one year in prison.

1977–1980 James E. Carter Administration

Executive Branch

☐ Debategate: briefing book of President Jimmy Carter stolen and given to Ronald Reagan before U.S. presidential election, 1980

☐ Bert Lance (D), Director of OMB, resigned amid allegations of misuse of funds during the sale of a Georgia bank to BCCI. No charges were ever filed. (1977)

Legislative Branch

☐ Fred Richmond (D-NY)—Convicted of tax fraud and possession of marijuana. Served 9 months in prison. Charges of soliciting sex from a 16-year-old boy were dropped after he submitted to counseling. (1978)

☐ Charles Diggs (D-MI), convicted on 29 charges of mail fraud and filing false payroll forms which formed a kickback scheme with his staff. Sentenced to 3 years. (1978)

☐ Herman Talmadge Senator (D-GA), On October 11, 1979 Talmadge was denounced by the Senate for "improper financial conduct." He failed to be re-elected. (1979)

☐ Michael Myers (D-PA) Received suspended six-month jail term after pleading no contest to disorderly conduct charged stemming from an incident at a Virginia bar in which he allegedly attacked a hotel security guard and a cashier.

☐ Charles H. Wilson (D-CA) censured after he converted $25,000 in campaign funds to his own use and accepted $10,500 from a man with a direct interest in legislation before Congress. This was a later non-Park incident.

☐ John Connally (R-TX), Milk Money scandal. Accused of accepting a $10K bribe. He was acquitted. (1975)

☐ Richard Tonry (D-LA) pleaded guilty to receiving illegal campaign contributions.

☐ Koreagate scandal involving alleged bribery of more than 30 members of Congress by the South Korean government represented by Tongsun Park. Several other Koreans and Congressmen were allegedly involved, but not charged or reprimanded. The most notable are:

1. Richard T. Hanna (D-CA) pleaded guilty and sentenced to 6–30 months in federal prison. [228] Wound up serving a year in prison.

2. Otto E. Passman (D-LA) was accused of bribery and other charges, but found innocent.

3. John J. McFall, Edward Roybal, and Charles H. Wilson, all (D-CA). Roybal was censured and Wilson was reprimanded, while McFall was reprimanded.

1974–1976 Gerald Ford Administration
Executive Branch

☐ Nixon pardon: The pardon by President Gerald Ford (R) of former President Richard Nixon (R), (who had appointed Ford his vice-president), just before Nixon could be tried by the Congress for conspiracy and impeached for his role in the Watergate scandal. (1974)

☐ Earl Butz (R) Secretary of Agriculture When asked privately why the party of Lincoln was not able to attract more blacks. Butz replied: "I'll tell you what the coloreds want. It's three things: first, a tight pussy; second, loose shoes; and third, a warm place to shit." Butz resigned soon after. (1976)

Legislative Branch

☐ Andrew J. Hinshaw (R-CA) Congressman convicted of accepting bribes while Assessor of Orange County. He served one year in prison. (1977)

☐ Wayne L. Hays (D-OH), resigned from Congress after hiring and promoting his mistress, Elizabeth Ray. (1976)

☐ Henry Helstoski (D-NJ) Indicted on charges of accepting bribes to aid immigrants but the case was dismissed by the Supreme Court. (1976)

☐ James F. Hastings (R-NY), convicted of kickbacks and mail fraud. Took money from his employees for personal use. Served 14 months at Allenwood penitentiary. (1976)

☐ Robert L. F. Sikes (D-FL) reprimanded for conflict of interest in failing to disclose stock holdings.

☐ John V. Dowdy (D-TX), Served 6 months in prison for perjury. (1973)

☐ Bertram Podell (D-NY), pleaded guilty to conspiracy and conflict of interest. He was fined $5,000 and served four months in prison. (1974)

☐ Frank Brasco (D-NY) Sentenced to three months in jail and fined $10,000 for conspiracy to accept bribes from a reputed Mafia figure who sought truck leasing contracts from the Post Office and loans to buy trucks.

☐ Frank Clark (D-PA) Paid congressional salaries to 13 Pennsylvania residents who performed no official duties.

Judicial Branch

☐ Otto Kerner, Jr. (D) Resigned as a judge of the U.S. Court of Appeals for the Seventh Circuit after conviction for bribery, mail fraud and tax evasion while Governor of Illinois. He was sentenced to 3 years in prison and fined $50,000. (1974)

1969–1974 Richard M. Nixon Administration

Executive Branch

☐ Spiro Agnew Vice-President (R-MD) to Richard Nixon was convicted of tax fraud stemming from bribery charges in Maryland and forced to resign. Nixon replaced him as V.P. with Gerald R. Ford (R-MI). (1973)

☐ Bebe Rebozo (R) investigated for accepting large contribution to Nixon campaign. No charges were filed. (1973)

☐ Watergate (1972–1973) Republican 'bugging' of the Democratic Party National Headquarters at the Watergate Hotel led to a burglary which was discovered. The cover up of the affair by President Richard Nixon (R) and his staff resulted in 69 government officials being charged and 48 pleading guilty. Eventually, Nixon resigned his position.

1. John N. Mitchell (R) Attorney General of the United States, convicted of perjury.

2. Richard Kleindienst (R) Attorney General, found guilty of "refusing to answer questions" given one month in jail.

3. Jeb Stuart Magruder (R) Head of Committee to Re-elect the President, pled guilty to 1 count of conspiracy, August 1973.

4. Frederick C. LaRue (R) Advisor to John Mitchell, convicted of obstruction of justice.

5. H. R. Haldeman (R) Chief of Staff for Nixon, convicted of perjury

6. John Ehrlichman (R) Counsel to Nixon, convicted of perjury.

7. Egil Krogh Jr. (R) Aid to John Ehrlichman, sentenced to 6 months.

8. John W. Dean III (R) Counsel to Nixon, convicted of obstruction of justice.

9. Dwight L. Chapin (R) Deputy Assistant to Nixon, convicted of perjury.

10. Herbert W. Kalmbach (R) personal attorney to Nixon, convicted of illegal campaigning.

11. Charles W. Colson (R) Special Counsel to Nixon, convicted of obstruction of justice.

12. Herbert L. Porter (R) Aid to the Committee to Re-elect the President. Convicted of perjury.

13. G. Gordon Liddy (R) Special Investigations Group, convicted of burglary.

14. E. Howard Hunt (R) 'security consultant,' convicted of burglary.

15. James W. McCord Jr. (R) guilty of six charges of burglary, conspiracy and wiretapping.

16. Virgilio Gonzalez guilty of burglary.

17. Bernard Barker guilty of burglary.

18. Eugenio Martinez guilty of burglary.

19. Frank Sturgis guilty of burglary.

☐ Pentagon Papers Exposed unconstitutional actions and coverup by Presidents Lyndon B. Johnson (D) and Richard Nixon (R) in Vietnam, Cambodia, and Laos from 1964 through 1971.

☐ Richard Helms, Head of the CIA, denied his role in the overthrow of Chilean President Salvador Allende and was convicted of perjury. He also destroyed all record of over 150 CIA mind control experiments of the MKULTRA project for which he was not prosecuted.

Legislative Branch

☐ Cornelius Gallagher (D-NJ) pleaded guilty to tax evasion, and served two years in prison.

☐ J. Irving Whalley (R-PA) Received suspended three-year sentence and fined $11,000 in 1973 for using mails to deposit staff salary kickbacks and threatening an employee to prevent her from giving information to the FBI.

☐ Martin B. McKneally (R-NY) Placed on one-year probation and fined $5,000 in 1971 for failing to file income tax return. He had not paid taxes for many years prior.

☐ Richard T. Hanna (D-CA), convicted in an influence-buying scandal. (1974)

Judicial Branch

☐ Harold Carswell (R): Was not nominated to the U.S. Supreme Court (1970) after publication of a 20-year-old speech: "I yield to no man…in the firm, vigorous belief in the principles of white supremacy." Was also alleged to be hostile to women's rights. Roman Hruska (Republican, Nebraska) defended Carswell by stating:

"Even if he were mediocre, there are a lot of mediocre judges and people and lawyers. They are entitled to a little representation, aren't they, and a little chance? We can't have all Brandeises, Frankfurters and Cardozos." Later arrested in (1976) for homosexual advances in a men's washroom.

☐ Harold Carswell Judge (R): Was nominated to the U.S. Supreme Court (1970) by Richard Nixon, but was not confirmed. Civil-rights advocates questioned his civil rights record, citing his voiced support for racial segregation during his unsuccessful election bid in 1948. Various feminists, including Betty Friedan, testified before the Senate, opposed his nomination and contributed to his defeat.

Roman Hruska (Republican, Nebraska) stated:

"Even if he were mediocre, there are a lot of mediocre judges and people and lawyers. They are entitled to a little representation, aren't they, and a little chance? We can't have all Brandeises, Frankfurters and Cardozos."

1963–1968 Lyndon B. Johnson Administration

Executive Branch

☐ Bobby Baker (D), adviser to President Lyndon B. Johnson: resigned after charges of favoritism. (1963)

☐ Billy Sol Estes (D): convicted felon who donated to Lyndon Johnson and influenced Texas elections. (1961)

Legislative Branch

☐ Ted Kennedy Senator (D-MA) drove his car into the channel between Chappaquiddick Island and Martha's Vineyard, killing passenger Mary Jo Kopechne. Kennedy pleaded guilty to leaving the scene of an accident and received a suspended sentence of two months. (1969)

☐ Thomas J. Dodd, Senator (D-CT): Censured by the Senate for financial misconduct. (1967)

☐ Adam Clayton Powell, Jr. (D-NY): was expelled from Congress but won the special election as his own replacement. (1967)

☐ Daniel Brewster (D-MD) Senator pleaded no contest to accepting an illegal gratuity in 1975 and fined $10,000. Brewster was convicted in 1972 of accepting $14,500 from a lobbyist, and got a six-year term in 1973 over the conviction, but the conviction was overturned on grounds of unclear jury instructions.

Judicial Branch

☐ Abe Fortas, U.S. Supreme Court Justice (D): resigned when he was discovered to be a paid consultant to a convicted criminal. No charges were ever filed. (1969)

1961–1963 John F. Kennedy Administration
Legislative Branch

☐ Thomas F. Johnson (D-MD) In 1962, he was indicted on charges of members of Maryland's S&L industry bribing him and lost his seat. Later was convicted of conspiracy and conflict of interest in 1968, served 3 1/2 months of a 6-month sentence and was fined $5,000.

☐ Frank Boykin (D-AL) Was placed on six months' probation in 1963 following conviction in a case involving a conflict of interest and conspiracy to defraud the government. His prison sentence was suspended on age and health grounds and was fined $40,000 total. He was pardoned by President Lyndon Johnson in 1965.

1953–1960 Dwight D. Eisenhower Administration
Executive Branch

☐ Richard Nixon (R): Eisenhower's V-P nominee delivers "Checkers Speech," to deflect scandal about $18,000 in gifts, maintaining the only personal gift he had received was a dog. (1952)

☐ (Llewelyn) Sherman A. Adams (R), Chief of Staff to President Dwight Eisenhower. Cited for Contempt of Congress and forced to resign because he refused to answer questions about an oriental rug and vicuna coat given to his wife. (1958)

Legislative Branch

☐ McCarthyism: A broad political and cultural purge against people suspected of sympathy with communism, starting near the end of World War II and reaching its climax in the investigations of Sen. Joseph McCarthy. The Senate passed a resolution of condemnation against McCarthy in 1954 after an embarrassing investigation of the United States Army, ending his career, but anti-communist purges continued for several years.

☐ Thomas J. Lane (D-MA) convicted for evading taxes on his congressional income. Served 4 months in prison, but was reelected three more times before his 1962 defeat due to redistricting. (1956)

☐ Ernest K. Bramblett (R-CA) Received a suspended sentence and a $5,000 fine in 1955 for making false statements in connection with payroll padding and kickbacks from congressional employees.

1945–1952 Harry S. Truman Administration

Executive Branch

☐ A Justice Department investigation of the Internal Revenue Service led to the firing or resignation of 166 lower level employees causing President Harry Truman (D) to be stained with charges of corruption. (1950)

Legislative Branch

☐ Walter E. Brehm (R-OH) convicted of accepting contributions illegally from one of his employees. Received a 15 month suspended sentence and a $5,000 fine.

☐ J. Parnell Thomas (R-NJ): a member of the House Committee on Un-American Activities (HUAC), was convicted of salary fraud and given an 18-month sentence and a fine, resigning from Congress in 1950. He was imprisoned in Danbury Prison with two of the Hollywood Ten he had helped put there. After serving his 18 months he was pardoned by Truman (D) in 1952.

☐ Andrew J. May (D-KY) Convicted of accepting bribes in 1947 from a war munitions manufacturer. Was sentenced to 9 months in prison, after which he was pardoned by Truman (D) in 1952.

☐ James Michael Curley (D-MA) was sentenced to 6–18 months on mail fraud and spent five months in prison before his sentence was commuted by President Truman. (1947)

1933–1945 Franklin Delano Roosevelt Administration

Legislative Branch

☐ Francis Henry Shoemaker (Farmer-Labor-MN) was sentenced to a year and a day in the penententiary for sending scurrilous and defamatory materials through the mail. (1933)

☐ Marion Zioncheck (D-WA) Killed after he jumped or was possibly pushed out a window in Seattle, WA while still in office. He was known to have been feuding with J. Edgar Hoover. (1936)

☐ John H. Hoeppel (D-CA), convicted of trying to sell an appointment to the West Point Military Academy. (1936)

Judicial Branch

☐ Halsted Ritter (R) U.S. District Judge of Florida, impeached for secretly taking a $4,500 fee from a former law partner. Convicted of bringing the judiciary into disrepute (accepting free meals and lodging during receivership proceedings.) Removed from office. (1936)

1929–1932 Herbert Hoover Administration

Legislative Branch

☐ Hiram Bingham Senator (R-CT) Censured for hiring to his staff a lobbyist employed by a manufacturing organization. (1929)

1923–1928 Calvin Coolidge Administration

☐ George English (D) U.S. District Judge of Illinois, impeached for taking an interest-free loan from a bank of which he was director. Resigned before his Senate trial. (1926)

1921–1923 Warren G. Harding Administration

Executive Branch

☐ Warren G. Harding (R-OH) President 1921–1923. His administration was marred by scandals stemming from men in his administration who followed him from Ohio who came to be known as the Ohio Gang. They include:

1. Albert Fall (R-NM) Secretary of the Interior who was bribed by Harry F. Sinclair for control of the Teapot Dome federal oil reserves in Wyoming. He was the first U.S. cabinet member to ever be convicted; he served two years in prison. (1922)

2. Edwin C. Denby (R-MI), Secretary of the Navy: resigned for his part in the Teapot Dome oil reserve scandal.

3. Harry M. Daugherty (R-OH), Attorney General: resigned on March 28, 1924, because of an investigation about a bootlegging kickback

scheme by his chief aide Jess Smith. Found not guilty. (1924)

4. Jess Smith (R) aid to Attorney General Daugherty (R) who destroyed incriminating papers and then committed suicide.

5. Charles R. Forbes (R) appointed by Harding as the first director of the new Bureau of Veterans Affairs. After constructing and modernizing VA hospitals, he was convicted of bribery and corruption and sentenced to two years in jail.

6. Charles Cramer (R) Forbes' general counsel, committed suicide. (1923)

7. Thomas W. Miller (R-DE), Head of the Office of Alien Property: convicted of fraud by selling valuable German patents seized after World War I for far below market price as well as bribery. Served 18 months.

Legislative Branch

☐ Thomas L. Blanton (D-TX) censured for inserting obscene material into the congressional record. According to Franklin Wheeler Mondell (R-WY) the letter was said to contain language that was "unspeakable, vile, foul, filthy, profane, blasphemous and obscene." A motion to expel him failed by 8 votes. (1921)

1913–1920 Woodrow Wilson Administration

Executive Branch

☐ Newport Sex Scandal: Assistant Secretary of the Navy Franklin D. Roosevelt initiated an investigation into allegations of "immoral conduct" (homosexuality) at the Naval base in Newport, Rhode Island. After the report, the investigators themselves were also accused of homosexuality. (1919)

1909–1912 William Howard Taft Administration
Legislative Branch

☐ William Lorimer Senator (R-IL), The 'blond boss of Chicago' was expelled from the U.S. Senate in 1912 for accepting bribes.

☐ Benjamin R. Tillman Senator (D-SC) and John McLaurin, Senator (D-SC) were both censured for fighting in the Senate chamber.

☐ Ralph Cameron Senator (R-AZ) attempted to control access to the Grand Canyon by buying mining rights to adjacent lands. (1912)

Judicial Branch

☐ Robert Archbald (R) U.S. Commerce Court Judge of Pennsylvania, for corrupt alliances with coal mine workers and railroad officials. Convicted and removed from office. (1912)

1900–1908 Theodore Roosevelt Administration
Legislative Branch

☐ John Hipple Mitchell Senator (R-OR) was involved with the Oregon land fraud scandal, for which he was indicted and convicted while a sitting U.S. Senator. (1905)

☐ Joseph R. Burton Senator (R-KS) was convicted of bribery in 1904 on the charge of illegally receiving compensation for services rendered before a federal department and served five months in prison. (1904)

1878–1898

Executive Branch

☐ Nehemiah G. Ordway (R) Governor of Dakota Territory was removed by President Chester A. Arthur after he was indicted for corruption. (1884)

☐ Ezra Ayres Hayt, Commissioner of Indian Affairs under Rutherford B. Hayes was forced to resign by Secretary of Interior Carl Schurz due to allegations of rampant corruption. (1880)

Legislative Branch

☐ Stephen W. Dorsey, Senator (R-AR) was included in the investigation of corruption of Star Route postal contracts under the administrations of President James A. Garfield (R) and President Chester A. Arthur (R). (1881)

1869–1876 Ulysses S. Grant Administration

Executive Branch

☐ William Belknap (R), United States Secretary of War under President Ulysses S. Grant (R): Resigned just before he was impeached by the United States House of Representatives for bribery. (1876)

☐ Whiskey Ring: Massive corruption of Ulysses S. Grant's (R) administration involving whiskey taxes, bribery and kickbacks ending with 110 convictions. (1875)

1. Orville E. Babcock (R) personal secretary to Ulysses S. Grant who was indicted in the Whiskey Ring scandal and 10 days later in the Safe Burglary Conspiracy. He was acquitted both times.

2. John J. McDonald (R) Supervisor of the Internal Revenue Service. Convicted and sentenced to three years.

3. W.O. Avery Chief Clerk of the Treasury Department. Convicted.

☐ Sanborn contract: kickback scheme between William Adams Richardson (R) Grant's Secretary of the Treasury and John D. Sanborn. (1874)

☐ Black Friday (1869): When financiers Jay Gould and James Fisk tried to corner the gold market by getting Ulysses S. Grant's brother in law Abel Corbin to convince Grant to appoint General Daniel Butterfield as Assistant to the Secretary of the Treasury where he could then give them insider information. (1869)

☐ George M. Robeson, Grant's Secretary of the Navy, was admonished by the House for gross misconduct and corruption in relation to his dealings with Alexander Cattel. (1876)

☐ Salary Grab Act: The act that increased the salaries of the president, Congress and the Supreme Court. (1873)

☐ Columbus Delano Secretary of the Interior under Grant, resigned after allegedly taking bribes in order to secure fraudulent land grants.

Legislative Branch

☐ Crédit Mobilier of America scandal:

1. Oakes Ames (R-MA) bribed Congress with Union Pacific stock.

2. James Brooks (D-NY) also implicated; both were censured for their involvement. (1872)

Judicial Branch

☐ Mark Delahay U.S. District impeached for misconduct in office and unsuitable personal habits, including intoxication. Resigned before his Senate trial. (1873)

1865–1868 Andrew Johnson Administration

Executive Branch

☐ Andrew Johnson: President (I) Abraham Lincoln's vice-president, was impeached for violating the Tenure of Office Act. He was acquitted by one vote. (1868)

1861–1865 Abraham Lincoln Administrations

Executive Branch

☐ Simon Cameron (R): Lincoln's Secretary of War resigned in 1862 due to corruption charges. His behavior was so notorious that Congressman Thaddeus Stevens, when discussing Cameron's honesty with Lincoln, told him that "I don't think that he would steal a red hot stove." When Cameron demanded Stevens retract this statement, Stevens told Lincoln "I believe I told you he would not steal a red-hot stove. I will now take that back." (1860–1862)

1857–1860 James Buchanan Administration

Legislative Branch

☐ Preston Brooks (D) Congressman from South Carolina burst onto the floor of the US Senate and beat Senator Charles Sumner (D) with a cane until he was bleeding and unconscious while two others held the Senate off at gun point. (1856)

☐ Daniel Sickles (D-NY) shot and killed the district attorney of the District of Columbia Philip Barton Key II, son of Francis Scott Key, whom Sickles had discovered was having an affair with Sickles's young wife, Teresa. He was tried and acquitted in the first use of the temporary insanity plea. (1859)

1849–1850 Zachary Taylor Administration
Executive Branch

☐ George W. Crawford (Whig-GA) Secretary of War in the Cabinet of President Zachary Taylor (Whig) was the center of the Galphin Affair land scandal with the help of Reverdy Johnson (Whig) Attorney General and William M. Meredith (Whig) Secretary of the Treasury, in which Crawford defrauded the federal government of $191,353. (1849)

1829–1836 Andrew Jackson Administrations
Executive Branch

☐ Samuel Swartwout was appointed by President Andrew Jackson to the New York City Collector's Office. At the end of his term he had embezzled $1.225 million in customs receipts and used the monies to purchase land. He fled to Europe to avoid prosecution.

☐ Robert Potter: Congressman from North Carolina who resigned from Congress after castrating two men he believed were having an affair with his wife. (1831) Later, in North Carolina, he was expelled from its legislature for cheating at cards or for pulling a gun and a knife during a card game. (1835)

1817–1824 James Monroe Administrations

Legislative Branch

☐ Corrupt Bargain: supposed bargain by John Quincy Adams with Henry Clay. (1824)

1801–1808 Thomas Jefferson Administrations

Executive Branch

☐ General James Wilkinson: was appointed to be Governor of the upper Louisiana Purchase. He then conspired with Spain to get Kentucky to secede from the Union in order to be allowed shipping on the Mississippi. (1787–1811)

☐ Aaron Burr: New Empire (Southwest) Burr conspiracy (1804–1807) In which Burr allegedly tried to seize a large part of the Louisiana Purchase and establish his own country. He was arrested for treason, but was acquitted for lack of evidence. (1807)

☐ Aaron Burr: duel with Alexander Hamilton (1804).

☐ John Pickering, Federal Judge appointed by George Washington was impeached and convicted in absentia by the U.S. Senate for drunkenness and use of profanity on the bench in spite of the fact neither act was a high crime or misdemeanor. (1804)

Judicial Branch

☐ Samuel Chase Supreme Court Justice appointed by George Washington impeached for political favoritism and acquitted in 1805.

1797–1800 John Adams Administration

Executive Branch

☐ XYZ Affair: French seizure of over 300 US ships

and demands for bribes and apologies, led to a Quasi-War causing the US Congress to issue the famous phrase, "Millions for defense, sir, but not one cent for tribute!" Real war was averted by treaty. (1798–1800)

☐ Matthew Lyon (Democratic-Republican KY). First Congressman recommended for censure for spitting on Ralph Griswold (Federalist-CT). The censure failed to pass. Also found guilty of violating John Adams' Alien and Sedition Acts and sentenced to four months in jail, during which he was re-elected. (1798)

1789–1796 George Washington Administrations
Legislative Branch

☐ William Blount Senator (Democratic-Republican-TN) Expelled from the Senate for trying to aid the British in a takeover of West Florida. (1797)

1777–1788
Executive Branch

☐ Conway Cabal: movement or conspiracy to remove George Washington as commander of the Continental Army by Thomas Conway and Horatio Gates (1777–1778)

☐ Silas Deane: accused of mismanagement and treason while ambassador to France. Intending to clear himself of the charges he died suddenly, and the charges were eventually reversed or dropped. (1777)

Now, if you still feel that one party is better than another, you are certainly wasting your time reading this book. However, I do appreciate that you purchased it because the proceeds will fund my master's degree.

Mark Twain made his remark quite a long time ago; clearly political corruption is not only old news but also indigenous to the profession. But *we do not have to put up with it*!

Source:

"List of Federal Political Scandals in the United States," Wikipedia, http://en.wikipedia.org/wiki/List_of_federal_political_scandals_in_the_United_States, accessed **08/23/12**.

CHAPTER 14

THE LAST CASH COWS

Have you noticed how not only health care is expensive, but also education is now prohibitively expensive? Here in the United States the cost of health services is out of control and that is because of the continual abuse that we allow. For example, one of the culprits are torts. All these class-action suits have affected health care beyond anything we could ever imagine; I am sure that you have seen TV commercials in which they tell you that if you have had an adverse reaction to a medication you may be entitled to monetary compensation. Well, that is just one of many factors that have affected both our health care system and insurance carriers. Ultimately, we end up paying for all these costs along with the veil of research and development.

John Grisham's novel *The King of Torts* is the story of how some law firms initiate class-action lawsuits and how the compensations are beyond our wildest imaginations, while the actual settlements for the client remain dismal in comparison to the fees paid to these law firms. While the story is fiction, the plot is all too real. I highly recommend that you buy a copy and read it; John Grisham is, as you may already know, an incredibly talented author.

The cost of health care keeps going up, and government subsidies like Social Security, Medicare, and Medicaid have to institute increases to keep up with the cost. Ultimately, we are going to find ourselves forgoing health insurance and making payment plans to pay four our medical needs; this will erode any equity that we may have. The cost of malpractice insurance for physicians—assuming they have it—is also exorbitant, and like any other cost in any industry it trickles down to the consumer.

Now, let's go to that other cash cow that I mentioned above: education. The cost of living is constantly going up, and the cost of education is rising along with it. Having just graduated from Flagler College with my bachelor's degree, I can tell you firsthand that it is amazing how students are being slowly nickel and dimed. While Flagler is still a hidden affordable treasure as far as cost is concerned, *it is well worth it.* Some of the many aspects that make college so expensive are the cost of books, and making sure our children have money for incidentals if they go away to college and the list would go on and on and on.

When it comes to books, the bookstores are making money hand over fist. While there are other, less expensive book sources available on the Internet, there's no denying that book buying is an expensive prospect. For example, a business law book will run you about two hundred dollars or more—*used.* And when you sell it back, you will be lucky if they give you anything over fifty dollars—that is, assuming that they'll buy it back at all! One thing that truly exasperates me is that these bookstores will not think twice to sell you a book that they know they will not buy back and the only difference between a discontinued edition and a "new" edition is often only aesthetics. As if the cost of books isn't enough, there are all kinds of fees that the college or university will assess—for enrollment, for "application processing," and so on. If you are a returning student you will have a "reenrollment activation fee"; the list goes on and on. One would think that after the tens of thousands of dollars that you have ended up paying by the time you graduate there would not be a graduation fee, but there is.

The worst part is that if you are going to attend graduate school, get ready to pay through the nose just for the entrance exam. I paid $75 to take the GRE, but due to circumstances beyond my control I had to reschedule and I wanted to reschedule it for two or three months later. Well, there was a rescheduling fee of $50, but since my rescheduling was for more than two weeks away the fee would be $175. I was so irate about this that I have decided to look for universities that do not require an entrance exam; I found several—and guess what—they are regionally accredited too.

What really gets my goat is that many of these institutions receive grants from the US government; we are talking about millions of dollars that come from our tax contributions! So we pay when we enroll, plus all the ancillary fees and then again through our tax dollars regardless if we attend or not; when does it end?

Luckily, when our son was born our financial adviser told us to just invest in mutual funds every month, which we have done, and so far it has outpaced any college prepaid plan. The beauty of this is that should our son earn a scholarship (he has earned straight As, thanks to my wife and his determination) or end up going to the US Air Force Academy, which he has expressed interest in doing, the money we have saved in mutual funds is ours, with all its capital appreciation.

By comparison, if you go with one of these prepaid plans, you will be lucky if you get back the interest should your son or daughter not need the plan; more likely you will get the principal balance without any gains, or if you are lucky with a dismal interest rate that would not even come close to offsetting the rate of inflation. Some of these plans will even restrict where the child can attend—whether it's a private school, an in-state college or, God knows, whatever other covenants they might require.

Nevertheless, we must ensure that our children get their education. It is a known fact that a country's economic worth is directly correlated to the educational level of its citizens. I am fairly convinced that if we were to be better educated in the United States, we could shake off past and future recessions with greater ease. Innovation is directly correlated to education and research where new entrepreneurial ventures are commonly conceptualized. This, as you may know, will impel new industries and/or enhance current industries to new heights and new levels of economic development.

For that reason, we cannot shortchange education. However, our government can throw all the money it has into education, but it will not make a difference if parents do not become vested in their children's schooling. Granted, this is easier said than done; our son would not be the straight-A student that he is if it were not for my wife's insistence and continual auditing of his schoolwork, as I am busy with school, work, and this book (to name a few of the things that keep me out of trouble).

Yes, there are those who have parents working different shifts with different days off where there is little opportunity to help with homework or other things. Nevertheless, we owe it to our children and to their future, which will in turn make our country even better. I say this because when I finished high school I did not see the importance of continuing my education because I wanted to have a good time and going to college was not the thing for me at that time. I could place blame on my parents, but the failure is my own. I always thought I knew what the best path was, and each time I came to a crossroad I more often than not chose the path of least resistance. Consequently

I realized I had a family to support and the only way I could achieve more income was to go back to school and earn a degree which I have done. However, my wife and I will not fail in ensuring that our son becomes the air force pilot that he wants to be and I frequently tell him that he will be the best pilot the air force has ever seen.

CHAPTER 15

PRIVATIZATION

For years we have heard of how much cheaper the private sector can accomplish things versus our government. Well, this effort was the main objective of former governor Jeb Bush in Florida, and as of today Floridians have yet to see these benefits; hence, the state is still cutting budgets and now with Governor Rick Scott we are facing more privatization notwithstanding the lack of evidence that proves that it is cost-effective.

Once again, all this is symptomatic of the comments often made about how incompetent our government is. If this was true, then why it is that most of the sectors that have been privatized have not shown any benefit to the state of Florida? Former Florida governor Charlie Crist even stated that the privatization efforts in Florida have yet to yield any savings when he was in office.

The late comedian George Carlin stated in one of his shows that "if there were to be any money made in helping the jobless and homeless then there would not be a single soul out there without a job or home [Sic.]." I could not agree more!

This is not to say that privatization in some areas can prove to be wise and efficient, as in the printing of government literature, though even that can be questionable at times. As it is, affluent corporations can afford to pay for political favors by financing campaigns; the end result is that they profit at the taxpayers' expense.

During the administration of the late Florida Governor Lawton Chiles, the state bought fleets of cars for "official use." Thankfully, one of the good things that Jeb Bush's administration did was to change that by selling the vast majority of the fleet and negotiating with car rental companies to provide the same services at a fraction of the cost of owning the vehicles.

It is commonly said that history repeats itself. Listening to NPR on my way to work on November 16, 2011, I heard that it had been discovered that Florida governor Rick Scott's aides employed a law firm to the tune of $400,000 for services rendered. The state paid fees of about $495 per hour when the state's allowable rate is closer to $100 per hour. Of course, just as in 1997—when Scott was implicated in the biggest Medicare fraud case in US history and had to step down as CEO of Columbia/HCA after the hospital giant was fined 1.7 billion dollars—he claimed he knew nothing about it.

A government's operational success is measured by the number of people it serves. Yet in the private sector the emphasis is the bottom line and not on serving the people. The fact will always be that private endeavors resist regulation. Regulation affects the bottom line, and I certainly can understand that, but our natural resources, our safety, and our interests must be protected. If the stewardship of our interest is left to the private sector, I assure you that we would not only jeopardize our liberties but would become yet another third world country in which there is no middle class and the gap between the wealthy and the poor could be measured in parsecs (an astronomical distance that is equivalent to approximately nineteen trillion miles).

This, as history has shown, is not the best position to be in as it lends itself to civil unrest where governments are toppled with violence. This is not to say that our government should provide us with our livelihood, as that would be socialism or communism. It can be said that our government has an infrastructure in place which is essential for our country's social, economy and military needs. History has shown not only how privatization does not work in many cases but also how it lends itself to even more fraud and other illicit activities that often make it to the media—and then we become outraged. In fact, I have mentioned in earlier chapters how governor Rick Scott's company (now his wife's company) was poised to do the specimen drug testing for state employees, and I would not be surprised that the drug testing for welfare recipients that he legislated is being done by this family's company—or at least by those with close ties to Scott.

What is interesting is that any type of legislation is usually accompanied by what is called an impact study that is purportedly by an independent entity and some officials of the agency requesting the analysis. One has to wonder if this was done for the drug testing that Governor Scott is legislating.

Currently, Governor Scott is spearheading legislation to privatize prisons. Once again Governor Scott, along with some of his legislative supporters, is pushing this without enough data or studies to justify the cost—that is, without a cost-benefit analysis. While driving to work one morning I was listening to NPR and heard that the Florida Legislature has elected not to continue with prison privatization until studies have been undertaken. I wouldn't be surprised if the governor and his supporters are going to find an "independent" agency (wink, wink) to conduct such study in an "equitable and reasonable manner" (wink, wink) to have a "fair and balanced" assessment.

Governor Scott's insistence on this issue really makes me wonder how much of a vested interest he has with privatizing jails. The vast majority of privatization that the State of Florida has undertaken in the past has yet to show any of the savings that it was projected to procure. Yet, the state wants to press on, and that should make you wonder what the motivation behind all this is; could money be the underlying motivation?

Sources:

http://www.examiner.com/article/did-you-know-gov-rick-scott-used-his-company-to-perform-mandatory-drug-tests accessed on 08/22/7013

CHAPTER 16

EDUCATION

I once heard from a man who emigrated from Cuba and who is a civil engineer tell me that one of the biggest ironies in the United States is that a person who swings a bat and hits a ball will earn millions of dollars, yet an individual who goes to school and earns a degree can barely make ends meet—assuming that he or she can even find a job.

Governor Rick Perry of Texas once said during a debate that if he were to win the presidency, one of the departments he would disband is the US Department of Education. However, as Karin Zeitvogel notes, "The United States has fallen to 'average' in international education rankings released by the Organization for Economic Co-operation and Development. America has received scores around 500 on a scale that goes up to 1,000: 487 in math, 500 in reading and 502 in science, according to the AFP [Agence France-Presse]."

One of my best friends, a retired army major, has always maintained that our country's "elite" do not want the masses to be educated in order to retain a well-stocked source of laborers. This became apparent with Governor Perry's comments and with the actions of many politicians who have close ties with "big business." In fact, my friend commonly calls our country "The United States of Corporations." "Major T.A.R.," kudos to you, as that is now crystal clear. And kudos to you too, governor Scott Perry, and also to you, governor Rick Scott, for cutting funding to the Florida Department of Education only to later return two-thirds of what you originally cut.

I am dismayed at the type of TV programming that is now being aired. My good friend "Major T.A.R." could never understand why more participation was recorded with *American Idol* than with political elections that will have far more effect on our lives. Even more startling are so-called reality shows like A&E's *American Hoggers*, in which a family makes a living killing—sorry I meant to say "harvesting"—feral hogs. I do not see the need to air this type of show, which could give the whole world the impression that we in the United States are still living off the land, as was the practice in the Old West. However, it does show one aspect that I agree with: the legal use of firearms by citizens.

This is not to detract from or stultify those who watch or participate in the show, but we are better than this; we need to project a better image of America and Americans to the world. As it is, comments like that of governor Rick Perry and actions like those of governor Rick Scott in cutting funding for education will only perpetuate ignorance. We need to put more emphasis and resources into our educational system and instill in parents the idea that they must be completely vested in their children's education; otherwise countless numbers of dollars can be thrown at education with nothing to show for the cost.

As radical as it may seem, perhaps federal legislation should be passed in which parents who claim dependents of high school and college age should only receive the full deduction in their income tax if their high school and/or college dependents earn a grade point average (GPA) of 3.5 or higher; if they earn a 3.0 to 3.49 GPA, then the parents would be entitled to get only 25 percent of the deduction, and no deduction if the dependents have a GPA lower than 3.0. Special needs children would be the exception, of course. Ostensibly, this would put the parents in a position of accountability if they want the tax deduction. It might actually help the dependents earn scholarships and become part of our country's strength and future. Education *should* be fully funded for everyone, but parents must do their part; then the system, even with all its faults will stand a better chance of producing a better-educated, and not just "average," America.

Being "average" in the world's rank on education has its costs. It forces companies to seek better workforces overseas: Springfield Armory manufactures some of its firearms overseas; Chevrolet manufactures the beefy Camaro in Canada; and countless other companies are doing the same. Granted, the cost of labor is lower in Canada, but take a gander also at that nation's educational ranking.

As parents, my wife and I have made it a point that our son should watch documentaries in addition to other shows that he enjoys (all of which are subject to our approval). Today, thankfully, he is selective in what he both watches and reads. Of course, we have also made it clear that he must go to college, as I know firsthand what the cost is if one does not have his or her education, having only just recently earned my bachelor's degree.

Research and development is paramount at any and all levels, and it cannot be done in what is known as a "Walmart economy." Yes, education is expensive, but it is a necessity; and with a well-educated population, America's future can be secured in many aspects.

We all have an obligation to ourselves, our families, our communities, and our country to seek knowledge and develop our analytical aptitudes beyond any measure. What's even more disturbing is the availability of what I call placebo degrees: bachelors, masters, and even doctoral degrees that are available through the Internet without taking any courses. There are a few people I've known since their days in grade school who boast about their education when I know for a fact that they do not have the discipline to read a novel, let alone to spend hours studying subjects like advanced math, business law, humanities, or any other subject. What is even more atrocious is that these companies offer transcripts to accompany these falsified degrees which you purchase without having to attend college. In essence you are buying a degree and paperwork to go with it to make it look as if you actually earned it. You can do Internet searches under "degree copies," or under something similar, and you will be astonished!

Finally, it is a true shame that ignorance is all too common in our country. L. Z. Granderson, who is a CNN contributor, has written an article titled "America's Problem: We're Too Dumb." As insulting as this title is, it does have its points. In an effort to bring you a piece of this story I have elected to cut and paste pertinent parts of the article for you here.

> "It's fun to laugh at the people who struggle with simple math problems or are unable to find any country we're at war with on a map.

> "It's all fun and games until you remember that elections have consequences, and that many of those people who said they could name the president—but not the commander in chief—will soon be standing in a voting booth, armed with a ballot."

> The good news is that we didn't finish last in anything.

> The bad news is that we're in pretty sad shape when not finishing last is the good news.

Trailing every country in the survey except Italy and Spain in math is rough. But how the OECD's findings may play a role in elections and the economy is disturbing.

According to the report, "individuals who score at lower levels of proficiency in literacy are more likely than those with higher proficiency to…believe that they have little impact on the political process." Also "in most countries, individuals with lower proficiency are also more likely to have lower levels of trust in others." U.S. adults ranked 16th in literacy proficiency.

An uneducated workforce is a hindrance to us all and an uninformed electorate is the thorn in democracy's side, taunting us with the words of Joseph de Maistre: "Every country has the government it deserves."

While it seems there's a chance we could be headed toward an agreement that will put an end to the partial government shutdown, we must not overlook the fact that the man most credited/blamed for the disruption was on the Senate floor quoting "Green Eggs and Ham" during his filibuster.

But this is not just a Republican problem. I can't help but notice the correlation between a more partisan nation and a more dumb-ass nation—regardless of party. Remember Ted Cruz is not the first politician to drag Dr. Seuss into the mess that is Washington.

In 2007, during the immigration debate, Sen. Harry Reid read a piece from the New York Times that contained quotes from "The Cat in the Hat."

When Gallup asked Americans what was the country's top problem, after dysfunctional government, the top-listed items were the economy (19%), unemployment (12%), the deficit (12%) and health care (12%). Sadly education didn't crack the top five, despite being the one area that really links them all.

"Proficiency in literacy, numeracy and problem solving in technology rich environments is positively and independently associated with the probability of participating in the labor market and being employed, and with higher wages," the new OECD report stated.

Educators will tell you the best catalyst for prolonged academic success is early childhood education.

Among the 38 OECD and G20 countries that participated in a report released last year, we were 28th in the percentage of 4-year-olds who are receiving early childhood education.

Hmmm, those late-night interviews aren't so funny anymore.

This article goes hand in hand with certain educational issues that hinder us as a nation to progress intellectually and to better our country.

Sources:
Karin Zeitvogel, "US Falls to Average in Education Ranking," http://www.google.com/hostednews/afp/article/ALeqM5juGFSx9LiPaur6eO1KJAypB2ImVQ?docId=CNG.5337504e8f65acf16c57d5cac3cfe339.1c1, accessed 11/20/2014.
L. Z. Granderson, "America's Problem: We're Too Dumb," http://www.cnn.com/2013/10/14/opinion/granderson-dumb-america/index.html?hpt=us_mid, accessed 11/20/2014.

CHAPTER 17

DEFICITS

It never ceases to amaze me how, ever since Barack Obama became president, the US deficit is now such a major issue for the Republicans. I distinctly remember watching Congresswoman Michelle Bachman in an interview with the Fox News network boasting a bar chart showing an immense spike in spending shortly after President Obama took office.

Well, first of all, the federal budget goes from October of one year to September of the next; therefore it is safe to say that when President Obama took office, that fiscal year was just over three months old and the budget had been devised by the administration of the previous president, George W. Bush. Additionally, the Bush administration kept all the spending related to the Iraq and Afghanistan wars off the books. The number of conservative supporters who concurred with Congresswoman Bachman's analysis is simply appalling.

In a nutshell, this is how it happened. When President Bush was first in office, he not only split up the entire budget surplus to each and every one of us in the form of tax rebates but also cut taxes. Well, this is very simple math: if you cut your income and increase your spending, the outcome is rather obvious. Then, to add insult to injury, the Republicans in defending this asserted that debt is a good part of any economy. Additionally, how often were the spending caps increased during the administrations of George W. Bush and Bill Clinton; yet in recent budgetary sessions it has been a point of contention that threatened to freeze government operations, which it led to a government shutdown. We need to send a strong message to all politicians that they need to work together and stop the dog and pony show! The United States is *bankrupt* and needs to be fixed *now*!

In YouTube you can find a video titled "Bush Admits Iraq Was 'A Terrible Mistake.'" And—for what it's worth—in the video Bush even apologizes. That is all good and well, but we are now paying for his mistake, and the "wrecked lives" he references in this press conference. I am of the firm opinion that the Iraq invasion was solely to avenge Saddam Hussein's supposed plan to assassinate President George H. W. Bush, his father. Now that he has avenged this act, we are left with a very expensive mess and trillions of dollars of debt that you and I have to pay for through taxes. However, this pales in comparison to those who gave their lives and those who are scarred physically and mentally from the war; yet, our Congress holds our nation hostage with budget funding and government shutdowns.

There are two steps to digging ourselves out of the financial hole we are in. First, we all need to be better educated; second, we need to start paying taxes—and that includes corporations and the very wealthy, which must start paying their fair share. I do not directly blame the very wealthy for the loopholes that allow them to pay lower levels of taxes than do the poor and the middle class, but I am certain that they lobbied and financed campaigns to have such loopholes.

CHAPTER 18

AFFORDABLE HEALTH CARE REFORM "OBAMA CARE"

Perhaps the biggest contention we are witnessing is the Affordable Health Care Reform, also known as "Obama Care;" the fact is that since the Democrats support it, the Republicans have to oppose it. As I have mentioned before, I find it ironic that it is a constitutional right to own firearms and consume alcohol, but to have affordable health care is being contested beyond comprehension as an infringement of individual rights. Bill Maher said best in his show of 10/04/2013 is a mandate for a website to offer insurance by commonly known insurance carriers. What was amazing in this show was a video of people interviewed asking them what Obama Care is. The ones interviewed had no idea what they were saying; some even stated that it's a chip that is inserted in your arm to track your health care. Folks, it is just a website where you pick and chose you insurance from a host of insurance companies.

Yet, it is clear that the majority of Americans want Obama Care; last time I checked, Obama was initially elected based on his platform of the Affordable Health Care Reform. Additionally, he was reelected under the same platform, Health Care Reform; it was taken to the Supreme Court and found to be "Constitutional." Today, 09/27/2013, our Republican leaders are entrenched in a battle to rescind the Affordable Health Care Act; even after more than forty some odd attempts they still continue the battle. What is even more egregious is that Former Republican Presidential Candidate, Mr. Mitt Romney, who is the 70th Governor of Massachusetts, enacted during his administration a very similar health care legislation.

While I do not agree with the shutdown of our Government, I blame EVERYONE in Congress and President Obama! Granted, Senator Ted Cruz spearheaded this government shutdown along with other Tea Party Republicans; everyone in congress and President Obama knew what was coming and did not even prepare for this mess. Consequently we are seeing what happens when there is a small government and everyone is up in arms. So, if you want to see what small, to no government is wonder no more; this is what a bucket size government looks like, a government shutdown. Is this what small government is all about and the Tea Party Republicans claim that they do not want the government closed, yet they preach smaller government and led us to a government shutdown…

What makes this even more egregious is seeing Senator Ted Cruz claiming accomplishment of the standoff; all he reminded me was of Saddam Hussein after the first Gulf War claiming that Iraq was victorious because it stood up against 28 nations. The only thing that was achieved in the shutdown was a glimpse of what not having government is all about. I assure you that if gerrymandering were to be illegal, there is a chance that we may not see such staunch Leftist or Extreme Conservatives.

I am a proponent of Obama Care, my wife and I have preexisting condition and the cost of insurance is prohibitive. Ironically, many of our allies have social medical care for their citizens and they are global leaders and prospering countries. A personal friend of mine is from Europe and due to the US's health care costs, he and his wife have had to fly over to Europe for treatment that in the US it costs them $25,000.00 per event. In Europe, they paid $2,500.00 USD for the same exact treatment!

Be cognizant of the fact, that even the commercials from the right depicting "Uncle Sam" as OBGYN are wrong. The Republicans do not want to get the government involved in health care, but some of the Republican presidential candidates even suggested that pre-marital sex should be illegal. So in a crude way, they don't want us to play with "it," but they certainly want to make abortions illegal; and yet, they'll send our sons and daughters to chase WMDs all over Iraq under false pretense, but they are against abortion! I guess they want a healthy stock of recruits ready to ship off to war.

This is not to imply in any way shape or form, that my views are correct; rather what I want to point out is the irony that abounds in our political sector. One thing, for those Tea Party Republicans that want to reduce the size of government and those extreme Liberals that want government to provide everything, why don't we start by laying them off, permanently, and not fill their vacancy? Lead by example; WHAT A CONCEPT!!!

One of the new Republican intellect, Ms. Ana Navarro said it best; "Obama Care it is the Law of the Land." Ms. Navarro is the best in-formed Moderate Republican that I have seen in a while and I am so glad that she is up and coming. I will say, however, she seems to be a fan of Jeb Bush and that is one of a handful of aspect where I find dis-agreement with her. Nevertheless, Ms. Navarro has many valid views that I concur with and she is someone worth listening to as she is very well informed. This is further evidenced by today's (12/11/2013) announcement of Florida Republican Senator Mr. Marco Rubio signing up for health insurance through the US Government's website.

Don't kid yourself; we have some forms of government medical services in the US Public Health Service and the venerable Veterans Administration. As a Disabled Veteran myself, I will tell you that I have yet to have any issues with the VA that I have not been able to mitigate with the aid of my senatorial representative; Sen. Bill Nelson.

Above all, please do not oppose the Affordable Health Care Reform just because the Republicans do; I have a close friend who refuses to even sign up because its "Obama Care." I have news for people like this, all you are doing is depriving yourself out of spite. My friend will not even research it simply because it has to do with Obama. Pssst, I have news for those of you who have this type of spitefulness, what if it is cheaper and offers more coverage? What makes this particular predicament interesting is that this friend has a pre-existing condition that would otherwise would not be able to get insurance in the first place if it weren't for the Affordable Health Care Act; "Obama Care." I assure you that if this is your way of thinking, President Obama and everyone else will not lose sleep over your reluctance to even sign up.

We need Obama Care, we need Medicare, Medicaid and Social Security and above all we need our Government. I have mentioned it before; our country's greatness is due to our people and, yes, our government! Do not buy into the idea that a smaller government is better, as large government is just as detrimental. However, you sit back and analyze all the things that the US Government monitors for our safety, consumption, protection I assure you that you'll appreciate the great job our public sector employees do.

As you know The Department of Veterans Affairs is being investigated for stratifying information regarding patient care. This is not typical of a "government" run entity. The fact is that there are count-less malpractice issues and patient data stratification in the private sector as well.

Just ask yourself how many malpractice suits have been settled out of court? We would never know as the documentation may very well require legal procedures. The difference is that government entities have to be open to public review of records, but in the private sector it requires a court order. As a Disabled Veteran I will attest that I have received top notch health care and have had the privilege to meet some of the best physicians whose interest is not what insurance you carry and how much they would make by providing certain medical services and/or procedures, but rather my health.

THANK YOU

In conclusion, I profusely thank you for reading this book and hope that you have been motivated to expand your knowledge and seek different perspectives for yourself. It does not matter what party you support, what matters is that you understand how and why you vote the way you do; we have to look at the whole picture and hope that we learn from the past.

The political paradox will continue regardless of how well informed we are as politicians will continue their marketing as their objective is to be elected/re-elected and those who provide financial support for their respective campaigns will continue to purchase legislative favors. However, if we all unite and speak against such actions, maybe, just maybe we can change things to better benefit us and our great country.

Let's do our homework and teach our children, as my wife and I have taught our son, to seek as much information as possible before making any decision. We need to stop picking the path of least resistance and exercise our analytical ability and weigh all our options.

www.ingramcontent.com/pod-product-compliance
Lightning Source LLC
Chambersburg PA
CBHW070423290526
45791CB00005B/1806